On the Dignity of Man

On Being and the One

Heptaplus

PICO DELLA MIRANDOLA
On The Dignity of Man

Translated by
Charles Glenn Wallis

On Being and the One

Translated by
Paul J. W. Miller
Associate Professor of Philosophy, University of Colorado

Heptaplus

Translated by
Douglas Carmichael
Professor of Philosophy, St. Lawrence University

With an Introduction by
PAUL J. W. MILLER

Hackett Publishing Company, Inc.
Indianapolis/Cambridge

Count Giovanni Pico della Mirandola: 1463–1494

Copyright © 1965 by
The Bobbs-Merrill Company, Inc.

Reprinted 1998, with new Bibliography, by
Hackett Publishing Company, Inc.

Printed in the United States of America

04 03   2 3 4 5 6

Cover design by Listenberger & Design Associates

Library of Congress Cataloging-in-Publication Data

Pico della Mirandola, Giovanni, 1463–1494.
    [Selections. English. 1998]
    On the dignity of man/Pico della Mirandola; translated by
Charles Glenn Wallis.
    On being and the one/translated by Paul J. W. Miller.
    Heptaplus/translated by Douglas Carmichael.
    p.   cm.
    Originally published: Indianapolis: Bobbs-Merrill, [1965], in
series: Library of liberal arts. With new bibliography.
    Includes bibliographical references.
    ISBN 0-87220-397-2 (hardcover: alk. paper).
    ISBN 0-87220-396-4 (pbk.: alk. paper)
    1. Philosophical anthropology—Early works to 1800.
2. Ontology—Early works to 1800. 3. Bible. O.T. Genesis I.
1–27—Criticism, interpretation, etc.—Early works to 1800.
I. Pico della Mirandola, Giovanni, 1463–1494. On being
and the one. II. Pico della Mirandola, Giovanni, 1463–
1494. Heptaplus. III. Title. IV. Title: On being and the
one. V. Title: Heptaplus.
B785.P52E5   1998
195—dc21   97-51631
                                                CIP

The paper used in this publication meets the minimum requirements of
American National Standard for Information Sciences—Permanence
of Paper for Printed Library Materials, ANSI Z39.48-1984.

∞

CONTENTS

INTRODUCTION

I

The Italian Renaissance is a phenomenon so complex and ambiguous that it eludes attempts at definition. The most obvious meaning of renaissance is rebirth, or more particularly, the revival of classical antiquity. But though many celebrated works of Renaissance architecture, sculpture, or literature are plainly inspired by classical models, they are not mere repetitions of classic prototypes, and in many fields, such as painting, Renaissance works are not imitated from ancient ones at all. Thus the revival of the ancient world seems to be only one aspect of the Renaissance. The persistence of medieval forms, techniques, and ideas is equally evident. But the culture of the Renaissance cannot be reduced either to an imitation of antiquity or to a prolongation of the Middle Ages, for the fifteenth-century Italian artists and writers created a new style in which a great variety of elements, derived from both ancient and medieval sources, are utilized in a new and original way.

Philosophy in fifteenth-century Italy displays characteristics parallel to those of art and letters. Philosophers exhibit a similar enthusiasm for classical antiquity, a zeal for the discovery of hitherto unnoticed ancient source material, a continuing interest in traditional problems formulated in a new manner. Furthermore, Renaissance thinkers could master and associate a great range of ideas in several different fields. All of these traits can be observed in the philosophy of one of the foremost intellects of the time, Giovanni Pico della Mirandola. His thought is not only of the greatest intrinsic interest, but discloses, through one individual, the spirit of the Italian Renaissance.

The vast scope and variety of Pico's intellectual curiosity and learning indicate the complexity of his philosophy. The list of books in his personal library, on which he spent much of his inherited wealth, has fortunately been preserved, and although he perhaps had not read all the books he owned, they provide an excellent idea of the sources of his philosophy. Literature, science, philosophy, and theology are represented in Greek, Latin, and Hebrew, with a few volumes in Arabic and Aramaic. Pico boasts, quite justifiably, that he has studied all schools of philosophy, and that his knowledge is not limited to any one tradition. The range of his erudition is also seen in the list of nine hundred theses which, at the age of twenty-four, he proposed for public disputation; the propositions are drawn from the most disparate sources. Further, Pico's studies at Ferrara, Padua, and Paris, and his later residence in Florence made him acquainted with all the chief philosophic currents of the time. These included Aristotle, the Neoplatonic philosophers, the Greek and Latin Church Fathers, the principal scholastic doctors of the thirteenth and fourteenth centuries, and through his Florentine friends, the works of Plato in the original. Pico had considerable knowledge of Hebrew, and some slight acquaintance with Arabic and Aramaic, which gave him access to Jewish theology, philosophy, and science. His eclectic erudition was the wonder of his contemporaries.

A closer look at the contents of Pico's library suggests that his learning had a definite form and center. Almost nine-tenths of his books are in Latin, the language in which Pico did practically all of his reading and writing, and the majority of them deal with philosophy and theology. Greek philosophy is represented in the original language, but Pico seems to have read most of the Greeks in Latin translations. Of his philosophic works in Latin, the greater number are by medieval authors. The subject matter and authors of the nine hundred theses that Pico proposed for discussion also reveal the great predominance of the medieval Latin tradition. Greek and Hebrew texts played an altogether peripheral role in his intellectual life. Thus, although the source material of Pico's thought is exceptionally rich, varied, and independent of the limitations of any one philosophical school, the composition of his library already suggests a basic characteristic of his thinking; namely, that he saw his new classical or Hebrew learning in terms of a definite frame of reference provided by the Christian Latin tradition. The variety of his library reflects his conviction that truth is not restricted to any one philosopher or theologian; yet, although the material of his thought is frequently new and eclectic, the form, or point of view which dominates this learning, is in many ways medieval.

II

Pico utilized this great mass of philosophical and theological material in accord with certain very curious views about the history of ideas. It is a commonplace of medieval thought that the philosophical conclusions reached by reason, and the content of religious revelation, are in agreement. For Pico, this concord of truth is embodied in the actual history of thought. He considers Greek philosophy and the Judeo-Christian scriptural tradition both as unfoldings of a single pious philosophy. Pico thinks that he is rediscovering the unity of a sacred theology revealed through both Greek reason and Christian revelation.

Greek philosophy, in this view, contains an occult, secret tradition of theological wisdom, running from Hermes Trismegistus, Orpheus, Pythagoras, down to Socrates, Plato, Aristotle, and later thinkers.[1] (Pico even had some misinformation on the "Egyptian" source of Greek thought.) A sacred religious truth was presented by these thinkers in allegorical form, hidden under mythological fables. Even Homer conceals a profound moral and religious doctrine in epic images. The Hermetic tradition had recently been put back into circulation by Pico's older friend Marsilio Ficino, who translated the entire *Corpus Hermeticum* into Latin. These Hermetic and Orphic writings, which are now known to be forgeries dating from late antiquity (mainly the first few centuries of the Christian era), were thought by the Florentine philosophers to be of immense age. They were supposed to contain a continuous occult the-

[1] See below, *Heptaplus*, Proem, p. 68.

ology, which Ficino and Pico unveil by symbolic interpretation. Even such presumably clear-thinking rational philosophers as Plato and Aristotle were seen as initiates in a secret tradition of sacred truth.

The Renaissance admiration for the mysterious may seem slightly puerile and affected, yet Ficino and Pico took their work of allegorical exegesis very seriously, for once the inner meaning of Greek religion, thought, and poetry had been grasped, they were seen as a natural revelation of the mysteries of theology. The wisdom of the Egyptians and Greeks was not merely human; it had a religious origin and history which need only be discovered by techniques of exegesis.

Such Renaissance thinkers as Nicholas Cusanus, Ficino, and Pico therefore often exhibited a tolerant eclecticism, an open-minded, receptive attitude toward foreign and ancient philosophies and religions. As previously suggested, this point of view had a perfectly definite metaphysical and historical basis: they believed that the content of these various views was in basic agreement, and that a continuous religious revelation ran through the apparent diversity of human cultures.

The texts of the other set of ideas which Pico made use of, the Judeo-Christian religious tradition, were also interpreted by methods revealing a secret, deeper meaning underneath the crude literal and historical surface. Of course both Jews and Christians had long given the Bible a symbolic interpretation. But Pico believed that he could reveal hitherto unnoticed depths of truth in scripture. For one thing, Pico had a philosophic view of the world, including man, according to which each part of the world is wholly present in every other part. It follows that a truth about any one part immediately reverberates through the whole, and discloses truth about every other part.[2] The very text and literary structure of the Bible is isomorphic with the natural and divine order which it describes. Scripture contains implicit symbolic truths for every branch of science, philosophy, and theology.

[2] See below *Heptaplus,* Second Proem, p. 77; Book II, Proem, pp. 94–95.

Further, Pico's study of Hebrew gave him some access to the
qabbalah, a Jewish tradition of allegorical commentary on the
Bible. He believed that this tradition reached back to Old
Testament times. It was an esoteric interpretation of the Law,
first revealed by God to Moses alone, then transmitted secretly
down to the present. Pico treats the *qabbalah* with more respect
than it perhaps deserves. In any case, its influence on his
thought has been much exaggerated. Pico merely utilized the
qabbalah as another tool in his symbolic method of scriptural
exegesis. He derived certain new materials from it, but his
fundamental method of Biblical commentary is in no way original. Allegorical interpretation had been practiced throughout
the Middle Ages, and Pico did not need the *qabbalah* to discover it.

Pico makes independent use of the Hebrew tradition. He
rightly points out that he is not subservient to it. Whatever in
the Jewish tradition agrees with the Christian Gospel he re-
tains; he refutes whatever in it is foreign to the Gospel. Pico
thus makes use of both Greek and Jewish sources of wisdom
insofar as he considers them to agree with his own Christian
philosophy.

III

Pico's method of interpreting Scripture can be seen in his
Heptaplus or *Septiform Narration of the Six Days of Creation.*
The principle of his interpretation is the identifying of the
truths of science and philosophy with Biblical doctrines. The
Greek and Latin Church Fathers, in their commentaries on
Genesis, had utilized the cosmology of Plato's *Timaeus.* Pico
follows very much in their spirit.

The created world, according to the usual medieval cosmology
that Pico uses, is divided into three chief zones, (1) the intel-
ligences or angels, (2) the heavenly bodies, (3) the corruptible
earthly bodies. Pico's commentary points out how this hierarchy
is present in Genesis, and how Moses already alluded in a hidden way to the facts of natural science as Pico understood them.

Biblical concepts also include or signify philosophic concepts. Moses has thus anticipated the findings of Greek philosophers regarding matter, form, etc. Further, the Platonic notion of man as intermediate between the physical and spiritual worlds is held by Pico to be equivalent to the Biblical notion of man as the image of God. Man reunites the multiple orders of creation just as God contains the diverse perfections of creatures in a higher unity.

The natural world, in this sort of interpretation, is a physical embodiment or model of philosophic and religious truth, not a mere symbol or metaphor of a supernatural order: nature actually embodies God's goodness and wisdom. The parallel between one part of nature and another, between man and nature, or between man and God, is not a poetic fiction but a real isomorphism or identity of structure. Man is the image of God in that he actually reproduces in an imperfect, copied way the perfections of his exemplary cause.

Pico intended this notion of imitation or representation in a realistic, not merely in an aesthetic or metaphorical sense. The permanent interest and value of Pico's view of nature comes from his seeing the physical order as a translation of philosophical and religious truth. In this way, physics, philosophy, and Scripture literally say the same things in different languages.

IV

Since it is impossible to consider all aspects of Pico's philosophy, we shall look at only two major topics, his philosophies of man and of being, which will perhaps disclose the essential character of his thought.

The Italian Renaissance witnessed a renewal of interest in man and his intellectual activities. This study of human culture may be called humanism in a loose sense. In a more correct and strict sense, humanism refers to the ensemble of literary and educational ideals of ancient Greek and Latin culture which were consciously revived and imitated in fifteenth-century Italy. Classical literature had of course continued to be studied and cultivated all through the Middle Ages. Historians are constantly discovering new "renaissances" in medieval culture, which simply indicate the continuous presence of classical letters throughout that period. Still, the Italians felt a new enthusiasm for the classical world, into which they projected all the perfections of an ideal humanity.

This Renaissance humanism was not a philosophy at all, but a cultural and educational program.[3] The humanists were men of letters who employed elegant Latin. They were familiar with certain philosophic concepts, but they were not philosophers. They furnish a plethora of moral platitudes, but not original philosophic ideas. The philosophy of man of such abstract thinkers as Ficino and Pico is altogether distinct and is not derived from the literary movement of humanism.

In fact, fifteenth-century philosophy and literary culture are in many ways opposed. At various times during the Middle Ages there had been analogous conflicts between cultural ideals based on Latin literature and on philosophical speculation. This opposition between literary humanism and philosophic inquiry as ultimate ends of human thought is the subject matter of Pico's celebrated letter of 1485 to the Venetian humanist Ermolao Barbaro. Philosophy need not be written in classical Roman periods, according to Pico, but may employ barbarous medieval Latin, the language of the schools of Paris. For philosophy aims at truth, not at the display of literary virtuosity; it is concerned with reason (*ratio*), not expression (*oratio*). Classical eloquence was wasted on the futilities of myths and fictions, whereas philosophy gives us truth about things human and divine. Pico doubtless derives this contrast between rhetoric and philosophy from Plato, who never tires of opposing the sophist, a virtuoso of persuasive words, to the philosopher, who searches for what is really true. Pico admires the medieval scholastic doctors, Albert, Thomas, Duns Scotus, whose philosophical wisdom written in incorrect Latin is superior to the

[3] See Paul O. Kristeller, *Renaissance Thought. The Classic, Scholastic, and Humanist Strains* (New York: Harper & Row, 1961), p. 10.

eloquent but false philosophy of the Roman poet Lucretius. This letter to Barbaro is a particular case of the opposition between a properly philosophic ideal and the cultural program of literary humanism.

The philosophies of man of Marsilio Ficino and Pico are humanistic on a philosophic level. Ficino was the first Renaissance philosopher to formulate a metaphysical view of the nature and place of man in the universe. He was the animating spirit of a loose circle of friends calling themselves the Platonic Academy, and he made the first complete translations of Plato and Plotinus into Latin. His own voluminous writings provide Renaissance thinkers with a view of human nature derived from both Christian and Platonic sources. Man is the metaphysical center of the universe, standing between the physical world of nature and the spiritual world of angels and God. Ficino modifies the hierarchy found in Plotinus in order to obtain a perfect symmetry, with man balanced between the natural and supernatural orders. He considers this placing of man to be in perfect agreement with Christianity, according to which man is the image of God living in the world of physical nature.

Pico's most widely known work, *On the Dignity of Man,* utilizes Ficino's *Platonic Theology.*[4] Yet Pico finds the previous view inadequate, and so unfolds his own philosophy of human nature. The most remarkable contribution he makes is his notion that the root of man's excellence and dignity lies in the fact that man is the maker of his own nature. Man may be what he wishes to be; he makes himself what he chooses.

This celebrated idea is often misunderstood by later critics who interpret Pico in accord with modern philosophies of absolute mind or will. Such interpretations are anachronistic. Pico is not a philosopher of absolute freedom come to torment us before the time. His view of human will is founded on his own perfectly objective philosophy of human nature.

[4] See Paul O. Kristeller, *Il pensiero filosofico di Marsilio Ficino* (Florence: Sansoni, 1953), p. 119. Trans. Virginia Conant, *The Philosophy of Marsilio Ficino* (New York: Columbia University Press, 1943).

Man has a definite constitution and place in the world, according to Pico. The chief zones of the created universe as mentioned before, are the immaterial angels, the material but incorruptible heavenly bodies, and corruptible earthly bodies. Man unites these three worlds in his own nature. He is not so much another essence as the union of the other three, a lesser model of the whole creation, a microcosmos. This rather trite notion is not a mere symbol or metaphor for Pico; man is made of body and soul, and so literally embodies or reproduces in himself both the angels and physical nature. Thus man has the intermediate place in creation, since he is constituted by the combination of the extremes.

Man also embraces the whole of creation in a further sense, in that he knows it. Any intellectual nature comprehends or includes what it knows. Since the human intellect extends to both spiritual and material objects, man's knowledge is another uniting of extremes.

Not only the created world, but also God is included in man, in that an image embodies and includes its exemplar. Human reason is lord over the senses similar to the way in which God is lord over creatures. One must be careful not to exaggerate the force of Pico's parallel between human reason and God. There is only a similarity of relation, or analogy, between the way human reason functions and the way God acts. They are both ruling in respect to a lower order of reality. Reason is not a god; it partakes of some of God's functions.

Although man has a definite place in the created world, he is not restricted to some limited form. He gives himself his nature, as a sculptor gives form to a statue. This does not mean that man is an absolute creator of himself, for the making activity of man operates upon potencies which are already given. God has granted to man every kind of seed. They grow as man cultivates them. This notion is as old as Aristotle, who maintained that the virtues are innate in man potentially, but need to be actualized through habituation. The context of Pico's affirmation of man's freedom shows that he is thinking above all of moral freedom, the ability to give oneself the character or set of moral habits that one chooses. Man can make himself into a brute, by choosing the life of the senses, or he can choose supernatural contemplation, which makes man partake of the life of God. Yet Pico is not suggesting that man is outside the definite structure and order of creation; rather, within this order, man selects his own moral nature. The transformation of man into an animal or into the likeness of an angel are symbols derived from Pythagoras and Plato, and represent the ethical choice between good and evil. The citations from Moses and from Plato's *Timaeus* indicate the relation of Pico's view to the Judeo-Christian tradition, in which man is the image of God, and to Platonic philosophy, where man gives himself the sensual life of an animal or the philosophical life of the gods.

If *On the Dignity of Man* emphasizes man's greatness, Pico's later *Heptaplus* remarks his insufficiency. The later work complements the earlier. Both regard philosophy, or natural contemplation, as preparation for higher theological knowledge. The end of man is to return to his first cause, God, where our knowledge is perfected.

Pico formulates this traditional religious notion in Platonic, and particularly Neoplatonic terms. In Plotinus' philosophy, the goal of any being is to return to its first cause. All things partake of a single circular life, descending from and returning to their first principle, the one beyond being. The purpose of all life and thought, in such a philosophy, is to lose all relative being in reunion with absolute unity. The scheme of salvation in Pico's thought is Christian and not Plotinian, but Pico uses Neoplatonic formulas in order to state his own views. For Pico, happiness is a return to God in that man conforms himself to and becomes a perfect image of his exemplary cause. This supernatural elevation of human nature is beyond the natural faculties of reason and will; they are perfected in a higher order by grace.

Pico had a very brief career. It seems most implausible that his writings would present radical changes of viewpoint; a much more likely interpretation is that his philosophy is a consistent whole. In Pico's view, the freedom of man, with its obvious echoes of Plato and Aristotle, is in perfect agreement with the insufficiency of this freedom to attain man's end, based on a religious interpretation of man. The natural order remains perfectly intact while enclosed within a further supernatural order. Pagan Greek philosophies, in Pico, retain their validity even when disclosing their final insufficiency. The concord of philosophies with each other, and with religion, is one of the most fundamental theses of Pico's writings. This agreement is embodied in the collaboration of man's free moral choice with a return to God which we do not make, but receive.[5]

V

Pico's metaphysics, though less widely known than his ideas on man, is equally significant for the history of philosophy. In his later years Pico was working on a vast *Concord of Plato and Aristotle*, which would have contained his metaphysics. The short *On Being and the One* is a portion of the uncompleted synthesis. It discloses the most fundamental principles of his thought.

Opinions have always been, and still are, divided on the question of the agreement of the chief thinkers of antiquity. Pico adheres to a long tradition of interpretation which maintains that Plato and Aristotle were really expressing the same philosophy in different terms. Neoplatonism, and practically all medieval philosophies, utilize materials from both ancient thinkers, a synthesis made possible by reinterpreting them. The original ideas of Plato and Aristotle are re-used, but in a new sense. This had been going on throughout the Middle Ages, although without benefit of most of Plato's original writings; their content was to some extent accessible through the indirect tradition. Pico was able to utilize all of Plato's works. As will be seen, his manner of interpreting them had much in common with the spirit of medieval philosophy.

The alleged disagreement between Plato and Aristotle cen-

---

[5] See below, *Heptaplus*, VII, Proem, pp. 150–151; and Letter to Gian Francesco, May 15, 1492.

ters on one fundamental point. Plato maintained that the one is superior to or beyond being. Aristotle held that the one and being were really the same thing in fact, and differed only in our mental concept or definition. Pico follows the Neoplatonic interpretation of Plato, according to which beings depend on an ineffable one beyond the many, definite formal essences. Being, or the realm of forms, is a second level of reality derived from the one. This region of formal essence is also identified with mind or intellect (νοῦς). Soul (ψυχή) is a third level derived from the second; it is mind temporarily present in matter. Finally, the world of physical nature is constituted by soul moving and working in matter.

This interpretation of Plato was widely held until very recent times. There is some evidence that such a philosophy, in which the one rather than being is the first principle, can be found in Plato's own writings. The Neoplatonists constantly quote certain favorite texts in support of their interpretation of Platonic philosophy as a hierarchy of emanations from the one. The good, identified by tradition with the one, is beyond being, but is the source of all being and intelligibility; the one is beyond all definite essence, being, definition, or description; truth about the highest principle is ineffable, beyond the distinctions of reason.[6] The Christian theologian Pseudo-Dionysius the Areopagite identified the Platonic or Neoplatonic one with the monotheist God. Emanation was reinterpreted in terms of creation, not to mention other appropriate improvements. In this Christianized form, Plato's thought exercised an enormous, though indirect, influence throughout the Middle Ages.

Marsilio Ficino, the first Renaissance thinker to know all of the original writings of Plato, continued to interpret Plato within the framework of the Neoplatonic tradition, pagan and Christian, which Platonism had acquired during the previous thousand years; the newly introduced Greek texts were read and understood by all the Florentine thinkers in this perspective. The very title of Ficino's major work, *Platonic Theology*, indicates its content. Although Pico's interpretation of Plato

[6] Plato, *Republic* VI, 509b; *Parmenides* 142a; *Epistle VII*, 341c.

differs in some respects from Ficino's, both Renaissance thinkers follow the long medieval tradition of the fundamental concord of the two Greek philosophers, transformed under the
influence of Christianity.

Pico's examination of the problem of being and unity was
occasioned by a discussion in which Lorenzo dei Medici had
maintained the Platonic view that the one was higher than
being. Lorenzo had doubtless been following the traditional
ancient and medieval interpretation of Plato's *Parmenides,*
adopted also by his friend Marsilio Ficino. Pico's *On Being and
the One* was written to show Plato is in merely verbal, not in
real disagreement with Aristotle, who maintained that the one
is convertible with or equivalent to being.

Modern critics rightly emphasize that the literary form of
Plato's dialogues often serves as a key to their philosophic
meaning. Pico was one of the first to remark this. He holds that
Plato, in the *Parmenides,* did not intend to assert any positive
theological or metaphysical doctrines, and that the structure of
the eight opposed hypotheses of the dialogue shows that Plato
intended only a dialectical exercise. It is a dialogue of method
and not of metaphysical content.

Ficino's interpretation had been influenced by the Neoplatonic emphasis on the first hypothesis of the dialogue. This first
hypothesis describes the ineffable transcendence of the one,
which is above and apart from all being and determination.
No being can be affirmed of or connected with the one. This
interpretation, which reads the opening hypothesis as a negative
description of the one as a pure identity beyond relatedness,
had gained added authority and plausibility from the commentary on the *Parmenides* written by the Neoplatonist Proclus.
The commentary breaks off at the end of the first hypothesis,
with the celebrated texts in which Plato says that the one is
beyond any positive being or definition. Any reader who interprets the dialogue more from Proclus' commentary than
from the dialectic of all eight hypotheses tends to conclude that
these are Plato's last and most profound words on the one.
Proclus' commentary had greatly influenced the Christian inter-

pretation of Pseudo-Dionysius, and, in its thirteenth-century Latin translation, had been read by the later medieval and Renaissance thinkers.

Pico's interpretation, that the first hypothesis of the *Parmenides* is no more important than the other seven, and that Plato's intent was not to disclose a profound metaphysical mystery, is based on a new emphasis on the form and method of Plato's dialectic. Pico has attempted to disengage Plato's original meaning from the misleading emphasis of a partial commentary. (Ficino, in his commentary on the *Parmenides*, begun in the same year as Pico's *On Being and the One*, 1492, replies that Pico's interpretation is "against the opinion of all the Platonists."[7] For Ficino, following Plotinus and Proclus, Plato's dialectical form is only an outer covering for a profound metaphysical content.)

Pico's reinterpretation of Plato bears on content as well as form. He shows that Plato's metaphysics is equivalent to Aristotle's by reinterpreting both, using notions derived from medieval philosophy.

Christians influenced by Plato identify Plato's one with God. The one is a pure identity; it is not another determinate being. What Plato says of the one can be applied to God, since God too is not another determinate essence or nature having certain formal characteristics. God does not have any of the determinations or properties of creatures. Pico attempts to show that, granted the identification of God with the one, it does not follow that God or the one is above being, in any sense which would contradict Aristotle. Aristotle's God, who is the highest or most perfectly actual being, is the same as Plato's. This identity is brought about by Pico's identifying both with the God of Abraham, Isaac, and Jacob.

In a standard medieval distinction, employed by Pico, being may be either (1) all that which is not nothing, or (2) that which does not lack existence *(esse)*. In the first sense of being, the things that are, and the things that are one, are exactly the same things. Aristotle rightly said that being and one are merely

[7] Marsilio Ficino, *In Parmenidem*, II, 1164.

two ways of describing the same things. Everything that is has both (a) being and (b) unity. Pico interprets Plato in such a way that Plato is simply assimilated to Aristotle on this point. Plato said that not-being was a principle of relative being, or otherness. Not-being enables beings to be different from other beings. So, in Plato, the many, or the not-one, or the different, are based on not-being. And if the not-one is not-being, then the one must be being. Plato is back in agreement with Aristotle's view that the one and being are the same.

Being in the second sense means that which does not lack existence (esse). That which is (ens) means whatever participates existence. Pico is here utilizing the metaphysics of St. Thomas Aquinas, who was the first Christian philosopher to base his metaphysics on the real distinction between that which participates existence (ens), and the act of existing itself (ipsum esse). (There can be no doubt that Pico derived his metaphysic of existence from Thomas. Pico's nephew, Gian Francesco, reports that of ten thousand propositions in St. Thomas, Pico disagreed with only three or four. Of the nine hundred theses Pico proposed for disputation at Rome, forty-five are taken from Thomas, more than from any other philosopher.) The doctrine of existence in Pico turns on the distinction, formulated by Thomas, between God who is his own existence, or is existence itself, and creatures, which are not their own existence, or, which merely participate existence.

The opening verse of Genesis states a religious truth which can be understood by philosophers in different ways. Creatures derive their very being from God. Some Christian theologians, influenced mainly by Platonic metaphysics, consider the distinction between God's being and the being of creatures to be chiefly a difference between eternal being and temporal being. St. Augustine, for example, constantly emphasizes the fact that God is eternally what he is, whereas creatures enjoy their being only transiently and temporally. God is, creatures are always ceasing to be, changing into something else. In a theology of Platonic inspiration, where being is thought of in terms of the self-identity of essence, God possesses eternally and perfectly the identity which creatures possess only imperfectly and for a time. In this sort of philosophy, God's giving temporal being to creatures is taken to mean that God gives them an imperfect possession of essence.

Other theologians, notably St. Thomas, pose the distinction between God and creatures on the level of existence rather than on the level of essence. The difference between God and creatures is that God is existence itself, or is identical with his existence, whereas creatures only participate or share existence. In God, there is no difference between what he is and his act of existing. In creatures, what a thing is, or its essence, is always really different from its act of existing. To say that God created the world is to say that he gave it existence. In this sort of metaphysics, the act of existing is not a mere mode of essence, or way in which essence is (for example, eternal or temporal). *Esse,* real existing, is the final actuality, really different from the actuality of essence, which perfects essence in a different and higher order. Creatures participate existence; that is what they are given in the opening verse of Genesis.

Plato had thought that particular individuals participate in forms or essences. St. Thomas utilizes this Platonic notion of participation in a new way. In his metaphysics, creatures participate not in some essence or manner of being, but in being itself. The difference between God and creatures is the difference between unparticipated and participated existence.

Pico della Mirandola adopts the solution of Thomas, even to the terminology. God is being itself, the act of existing, *ipsum esse,*[8] not another thing which partakes of being. He is being pure and simple, above the things which only have being. Pico takes from St. Thomas his scriptural proof; God tells Moses that his name is "I am who am."[9] Both philosophers take this to mean that God discloses himself as being itself. Other things participate existence *(esse);* God is the plenitude of unparticipated existence.

The apparent disagreement between Plato, who maintained

[8] *Heptaplus,* III, 1, p. 107 below; *On Being and the One,* IV, p. 44 below.
[9] Exodus 3:14, quoted in *On Being and the One,* III, p. 42 below.

that the one is above being, and Aristotle, who identified the one with being, can now be resolved. The one of Plato, now identified with the Biblical God, is above being in the sense that he is not another thing which has or shares in being. He is not a creature, not something that "is" in the second sense of "having existence" as an attribute. Beings are the things which partake of being; in this sense, God is above beings.

Aristotle held that being was divided into ten categories. God is obviously not a member of any one category; his existence is not a substance, nor a quality, nor a quantity, nor any other category. God is above the ten kinds or categories of being. And so, in Aristotle's view, as interpreted by Pico, God is above being. Plato and Aristotle agree that God is beyond being.

To an observer of the history of philosophy, it is evident that Plato's metaphysics is altogether different from that of Aristotle. Plato's view that being is a relation derived from the pure relation of identity, or the one, is incompatible with Aristotle's view that being means the concrete individual substance. Plato's good beyond being (*ousia*) is not Aristotle's God, who is the first or highest substance or entity (*ousia*). These two Greek philosophies can be made to coincide only when transformed into an altogether different philosophy: the highest principle in Plato turns out to be the same as the highest principle in Aristotle only because they are both identified with a God who is existence itself. God thereby embraces both the one beyond participated being, and the highest substance.

Pico's account of the metaphysical structure of the created world likewise shows a transformation of Greek ideas under Christian influence. The multiple world of creatures contains many natures, many beings, many kinds of good. Yet, while retaining their own being and goodness, creatures at the same time refer to a being and a good beyond themselves. The reality of things is both intrinsic, as in Aristotle's metaphysics, and also referential, as in Plato's. The created world has a double aspect. Creatures have their own being; they exist by virtue of their own act of existing. But this actuality is caused in them; they have it by participation, not by virtue of their own essences.

Because creatures have participated existence, they thereby refer to their unparticipated cause.

The same dialectic applies to the notion of the good. Each thing has its own goodness. But it has this good by participation, or, as caused in it by goodness itself. Thus creatures refer to goodness itself, the goodness of God, the way any effect refers to its cause. The good of a creature is in the creature itself, and yet, since it is caused, it leads beyond this instance of good to the good itself.[10]

The most fundamental possible way in which creatures represent or imitate or refer to God is just by existing. What they derive from God is existence, and so they refer to their cause simply by exercising that effect. Of course creatures also derive their formal or essential natures from God, but these are nothing until they exist. Just by virtue of the fact that a thing is, it both has its own being and has it as caused, or by participation, or as referential to absolute being. Plato's relational view of being is equivalent to Aristotle's philosophy of being as substance because Platonic participation has been reinterpreted as a sharing in being itself. Pico's concord of Plato and Aristotle, impossible within their philosophies taken on their own level, has been accomplished by transforming both into a different metaphysics.

This philosophy of participation in being itself has important consequences for the conduct of human life. Pico adopts the traditional Aristotelian view that the good and being are convertible, that is, they differ in thought or in definition but not in fact. Just as the being of man is both intrinsic and yet is a participation from God, even so the good of man has a double dimension. Creatures first attain their own intrinsic good. Aristotle rightly placed this in the proper functioning of a thing's own nature. Pico entirely agrees with Aristotle's view that philosophy, intellectual knowledge on the natural level, guides man to this purely natural or ethical happiness. Yet Pico regards this happiness as imperfect. The true end of each thing is to return to its first beginning, a Platonic notion which Pico

[10] On Being and the One, IV, p. 46 below.

doubtless read in Proclus. The supernatural happiness of man, the return to God, who is man's first cause, cannot be brought about merely by philosophical speculation. Aristotle's happiness on the natural level is only a preparation for the supernatural happiness of the return to God. The Neoplatonic notion of return to the one is assimilated by Pico to the Christian idea of divine grace which draws creatures to their Creator. Like Kierkegaard, Pico celebrates the father of faith, Abraham, because he was the first to rise from the level of nature to a supernatural promise.

This scheme of salvation is not a conventional set of pious platitudes but an integral consequence of Pico's metaphysics. In Platonic philosophy, the human soul is divine. It naturally inhabits the super-celestial place, the home of the gods. Plato regards the present life of the soul in the material world as only a temporary misfortune. Pico employs Platonic images to describe the different Christian situation. The human soul is not a god; it is an image of God, according to Pico. When Plotinus in his dying words announced his reunion with the one, he was speaking of the identification of the relative with the absolute, of the loss of human personality in the one beyond being. When Pico speaks of the return of man to God, he uses this language in a different sense. Man in his view becomes a perfect image of God, imitating in a human way the absolute unity of God. Like St. Augustine or St. Thomas, Pico re-uses pagan terminology to describe a dialectic which is similar in form to Greek philosophy, but entirely different in content. The divinity of man in this Christian philosophy does not suggest that man is a god. Man participates in the life of God both by his natural being and by his religion, which gives a supernatural life.

VI

Pico della Mirandola called himself an *explorator*. His explorations extended over the whole of philosophy, but were directed by a definite purpose: the discovery of the unity of truth in a harmonious philosophic and religious order, a unity present in a single historical tradition descending through Jewish, Egyptian, and Greek wisdom. Although the unity of truth can hardly be encountered in quite this literal and historical sense, we may still ask whether Pico the explorer found a new world.

The history of medieval philosophy is the story of the assimilation and reinterpretation of ideas derived from Greek philosophy. It is perfectly certain, for example, that the Christian Trinity is not mentioned by Plotinus, nor does Aristotle speak of a God who gives his effects their very existence. St. Augustine found the Trinity and St. Thomas found a God who gives being in Greek philosophy because they transformed it into their own original religious philosophies. These medieval syntheses opened new dimensions of philosophy hardly suggested in Greek speculation.

The Renaissance philosophy of Pico is a new episode in this tradition. The materials of his thought, particularly the works of the Platonic school, are often new. Like his "co-Platonist" Ficino, Pico understood these materials not in a strictly historical way, but in accord with his own constructive purposes. He was convinced of the unity of pagan and Christian thought. This agreement may or may not be encountered as a fact of the history of ideas. Pico created this unity by his own thought; the way in which he assimilated a great variety of doctrines conferred on them their common spirit. He saw the world of physical nature as a stage upon which truths of a spiritual order were embodied and represented. He read pagan literature and philosophy to find in it a prefiguration of religious truth. Scripture was an allegorical unfolding of mysteries. The convergence of all thought and experience, the agreement of philosophies, were, Pico believed, facts of history, but their unity was not merely empirical; Pico understood all aspects of thought and being as disclosing a common truth because they all proceeded from a common source.

Pico encounters in the world, in man, in the good or the one, a system of parts which constitute a unity. The principle of the relations of things is their common descent from God, their exemplary cause. The strongly symbolic, referential character of Pico's world is not based on aesthetic considerations, or on the ideal relations of thought, but arises from the perfectly objective, metaphysical unity which all beings have because they are effects of God, who is being itself. Similarly, in the order of physical and moral action, things come from the goodness of God, and return to it by natural and spiritual inclination. History, the world of nature, the conduct of human life form a whole because they all reflect in different symbolic languages a common providential source.

The materials of Pico's philosophy are characteristic of the Renaissance, and were in many cases unknown in the Middle Ages. His method of understanding these ideas, the form of his thinking, is religious. His thought is a new episode in the history of Christian philosophy.

The art and poetry of the Italian Renaissance have always been admired for the classic perfection of their forms, and the incomparable charm of their symbolism and power of suggestion. Although the secret of beauty remains unknown, much of the attraction of Renaissance works seems to lie in their suggestion of an ideal perfection beyond the particulars present to the senses. Yet this unity reflected by the multiplicity of things is not merely aesthetic. It is religious. Pico found new realms of ideas in his explorations. These new regions remain part of a single world, reflecting God as their cause. The philosophy of Pico della Mirandola expresses the fundamentally religious spirit of the Renaissance.

BIOGRAPHICAL NOTE

Giovanni Pico, younger son of the Count of La Mirandola and Concordia, was born in the family castle in 1463. He first studied canon law at the nearby university of Bologna, then, in 1479, attended the university of Ferrara. During a first brief visit to Florence that same year he met and made friends with Poliziano and other humanist poets, and in his early years, wrote Italian and Latin poetry himself, some of which he later destroyed.

Pico then studied philosophy at the university of Padua, 1480-1482, where he became thoroughly familiar with Aristotle and his chief ancient and medieval commentators, all in Latin translation. That university was known for the Averroist interpretations of Aristotle taught there, but this seems to mean little more than that philosophy was taught in connection with medicine rather than theology.

In 1482 he began the study of Greek. After further wanderings, in 1484 he visited Florence again, the city of the Platonic revival, and began there his study of Plato. The following year he went to the most celebrated center of philosophy, the university of Paris, but returned to Italy in 1486.

Pico began to study Hebrew, wrote his Italian *Commentary* to a poem by Benivieni, and, following the example of the scholastic disputes of Paris, proposed his nine hundred *Conclusions* or theses. These were written in the "language of Paris," that is, international scholastic Latin. The *Oration on the Dignity of Man* was intended as an introduction to the public disputation of the *Conclusions*. But the disputation never took place, having been suspended by Pope Innocent VIII. A commission found seven of the nine hundred theses heretical, and six more suspect. Pico wrote an *Apology* to protest his orthodoxy, retired to France in 1488, was arrested, and later released. His friend Marsilio Ficino invited him to come to Florence.

Lorenzo dei Medici provided Pico with a villa at Fiesole, where he spent the few remaining years of his life in retirement, in "the study of the liberal arts and sacred theology." Here he wrote his *Heptaplus* (a commentary on Genesis), 1489; various commentaries on the Psalms; *On Being and the One*, 1491; *Disputations Against Astrology*, 1494. He requested and was granted a full pardon by Pope Alexander VI. He died in 1494 at the age of 31, and is buried in the church of the Florentine humanists, San Marco.

SELECTED BIBLIOGRAPHY

Giovanni Pico della Mirandola and Giovanni Francesco Pico. *Opera Omnia.* Lubrecht & Cramer, 1969.

Giovanni Pico della Mirandola. *De hominis dignitate, Heptaplus, De ente et uno, e scritti vari.* Ed. E. Garin, Firenze, Vallecchi, 1942. (Has original Latin and an Italian translation on facing pages.)

————. *Oration on the Dignity of Man.* Tr. Robert M. Caponigri, Regnery, 1996.

————. *Of Being and Unity.* Tr. Victor M. Hamm, Marquette, 1943.

————. *Heptaplus.* Tr. Jessie B. McGaw, New York, Philosophical Library, 1977.

————. *Commentary on a Poem of Platonic Love.* Tr. Douglas Carmichael, University Press of America, 1986.

Cassirer, Ernst. *The Individual and the Cosmos in Renaissance Philosophy.* Tr. Mario Domandi, New York, Harper & Row, 1964.

Dulles, Avery. *Prineps Concordiae, Pico della Mirandola in the Scholastic Tradition.* Harvard, 1941.

Kibre, Pearl. *The Library of Pico della Mirandola.* New York, Columbia University Press, 1936.

Kristeller, Paul Oskar. *Renaissance Thought.* 2 vols., New York, Harper & Row, 1961–65.

More, Sir Thomas. *Giovanni Pico della Mirandola, His Life by His Nephew.* London, D. Nutt, 1890.

Winzanski, Chaim. *Pico della Mirandola's Encounter with Jewish Mysticism.* Harvard University Press, 1989.

————. *Renaissance Thought II. Papers on Humanism and the Arts.* New York: Harper & Row, 1965.

————. *Studies in Renaissance Thought and Letters.* Rome: Edizioni di storia e letteratura, 1956.

MONNERJAHN, ENGELBERT. *Giovanni Pico della Mirandola.* Wiesbaden: Steiner, 1960.

NOTE ON THE TEXT

The translations of *On Being and the One* and *Heptaplus* were made from the critical edition, edited by Eugenio Garin (Vallecchi: Florence, 1942), in the *Edizione Nazionale dei Classici del Pensiero Italiano*. Mr. Wallis' translation of *On the Dignity of Man* was made from a Renaissance edition, but has been revised by Mr. Miller to agree with the critical edition. A line of Hebrew printed incorrectly in that text has been emended by Professor Paul Shiman of the University of Colorado.

The translators are heavily indebted to the Garin edition for identifications of quotations and references to other works. In the *Heptaplus*, Biblical quotations and references are given as in the Douay version; in *On the Dignity of Man* and *On Being and the One*, reference was made to the Latin Vulgate.

On The Dignity of Man

A SPEECH BY
GIOVANNI PICO DELLA MIRANDOLA,
Prince of Concord

[handwritten marginal note: Why is man so great to think about?]

Most venerable fathers, I have read in the records of the Arabians that Abdul the Saracen, on being asked what thing on, so to speak, the world's stage, he viewed as most greatly worthy of wonder, answered that he viewed nothing more wonderful than man. And Mercury's, "a great wonder, Asclepius, is man!" agrees with that opinion.[1] On thinking over the reason for these sayings, I was not satisfied by the many assertions made by many men concerning the outstandingness of human nature: that man is the messenger between creatures, familiar with the upper and king of the lower; by the sharpsightedness of the senses, by the hunting-power of reason, and by the light of intelligence, the interpreter of nature; the part in between the standstill of eternity and the flow of time; and, as the Persians say, the bond tying the world together, nay, the nuptial bond; and, according to David, "a little lower than the angels."[2] These reasons are great but not the chief ones, that is, they are not reasons for a lawful claim to the highest wonder as to a prerogative. Why should we not wonder more at the angels themselves and at the very blessed heavenly choirs?

Finally, it seemed to me that I understood why man is the animal that is most happy, and is therefore worthy of all wonder; and lastly, what the state is that is allotted to man in the succession of things, and that is capable of arousing envy not only in the brutes but also in the stars and even in minds beyond the world. It is wonderful and beyond belief. For this is the reason why man is rightly said and thought to be a great

---

[1] *Asclepius* I. 6 (*Hermetica*, ed. W. Scott, I, 294).
[2] Psalms 8:5.

marvel and the animal really worthy of wonder. Now hear what it is, fathers; and with kindly ears and for the sake of your humanity, give me your close attention:

Now the highest Father, God the master-builder, had, by the laws of his secret wisdom, fabricated this house, this world which we see, a very superb temple of divinity. He had adorned the super-celestial region with minds. He had animated the celestial globes with eternal souls; he had filled with a diverse throng of animals the cast-off and residual parts of the lower world. But, with the work finished, the Artisan desired that there be someone to reckon up the reason of such a big work, to love its beauty, and to wonder at its greatness. Accordingly, now that all things had been completed, as Moses and Timaeus testify, He lastly considered creating man.[3] But there was nothing in the archetypes from which He could mold a new sprout, nor anything in His storehouses which He could bestow as a heritage upon a new son, nor was there an empty judiciary seat where this contemplator of the universe could sit. Everything was filled up; all things had been laid out in the highest, the lowest, and the middle orders. But it did not belong to the paternal power to have failed in the final parturition, as though exhausted by childbearing; it did not belong to wisdom, in a case of necessity, to have been tossed back and forth through want of a plan; it did not belong to the loving-kindness which was going to praise divine liberality in others to be forced to condemn itself. Finally, the best of workmen decided that that to which nothing of its very own could be given should be, in composite fashion, whatsoever had belonged individually to each and every thing. Therefore He took up man, a work of indeterminate form; and, placing him at the midpoint of the world, He spoke to him as follows:

"We have given to thee, Adam, no fixed seat, no form of thy very own, no gift peculiarly thine, that thou mayest feel as thine own, have as thine own, possess as thine own the seat, the form, the gifts which thou thyself shalt desire. A limited nature in other creatures is confined within the laws written down by

3 Plato, *Timaeus* 41b ff.

Us. In conformity with thy free judgment, in whose hands I have placed thee, thou art confined by no bounds; and thou wilt fix limits of nature for thyself. I have placed thee at the center of the world, that from there thou mayest more conveniently look around and see whatsoever is in the world. Neither heavenly nor earthly, neither mortal nor immortal have We made thee. Thou, like a judge appointed for being honorable, art the molder and maker of thyself; thou mayest sculpt thyself into whatever shape thou dost prefer. Thou canst grow downward into the lower natures which are brutes. Thou canst again grow upward from thy soul's reason into the higher natures which are divine."

O great liberality of God the Father! O great and wonderful happiness of man! It is given him to have that which he chooses and to be that which he wills. As soon as brutes are born, they bring with them, "from their dam's bag," as Lucilius says, what they are going to possess.[4] Highest spirits have been, either from the beginning or soon after, that which they are going to be throughout everlasting eternity. At man's birth the Father placed in him every sort of seed and sprouts of every kind of life. The seeds that each man cultivates will grow and bear their fruit in him. If he cultivates vegetable seeds, he will become a plant. If the seeds of sensation, he will grow into brute. If rational, he will come out a heavenly animal. If intellectual, he will be an angel, and a son of God. And if he is not contented with the lot of any creature but takes himself up into the center of his own unity, then, made one spirit with God and settled in the solitary darkness of the Father, who is above all things, he will stand ahead of all things. Who does not wonder at this chameleon which we are? Or who at all feels more wonder at anything else whatsoever? It was not unfittingly that Asclepius the Athenian said that man was symbolized by Prometheus in the secret rites, by reason of our nature sloughing its skin and transforming itself; hence metamorphoses were popular among the Jews and the Pythagoreans. For the more secret Hebrew

4 Lucilius, *Satyrarum* VI (22), in Nonius Marcellus, *De compendiosa doctrina* II (Lindsay, I, 109).

theology at one time reshapes holy Enoch into an angel of divinity, whom they call *malach hashechina*, and at other times reshapes other men into other divinities.[5] According to the Pythagoreans, wicked men are deformed into brutes and, if you believe Empedocles, into plants too.[6] And copying them, Maumeth [Mohammed] often had it on his lips that he who draws back from divine law becomes a brute. And his saying so was reasonable: for it is not the rind which makes the plant, but a dull and non-sentient nature; not the hide which makes a beast of burden, but a brutal and sensual soul; not the spherical body which makes the heavens, but right reason; and not a separateness from the body but a spiritual intelligence which makes an angel. For example, if you see a man given over to his belly and crawling upon the ground, it is a bush not a man that you see. If you see anyone blinded by the illusions of his empty and Calypso-like imagination, seized by the desire of scratching, and delivered over to the senses, it is a brute not a man that you see. If you come upon a philosopher winnowing out all things by right reason, he is a heavenly not an earthly animal. If you come upon a pure contemplator, ignorant of the body, banished to the innermost places of the mind, he is not an earthly, not a heavenly animal; he more superbly is a divinity clothed with human flesh.

Who is there that does not wonder at man? And it is not unreasonable that in the Mosaic and Christian holy writ man is sometimes denoted by the name "all flesh" and at other times by that of "every creature"; and man fashions, fabricates, transforms himself into the shape of all flesh, into the character of every creature.[7] Accordingly, where Evantes the Persian tells of the Chaldaean theology, he writes that man is not any inborn image of himself, but many images coming in from the outside: hence that saying of the Chaldaeans: *enosh hu shinuy vekamah tevaoth baal chayim*, that is, man is an animal of diverse, multiform, and destructible nature.

[5] Book of Enoch 40:8.
[6] Empedocles, fr. 117 (Diels).
[7] Genesis 6:12; Numbers 27:16; Mark 16:15.

But why all this? In order for us to understand that, after having been born in this state so that we may be what we will to be, then, since we are held in honor, we ought to take particular care that no one may say against us that we do not know that we are made similar to brutes and mindless beasts of burden.[8] But rather, as Asaph the prophet says: "Ye are all gods, and sons of the most high," unless by abusing the very indulgent liberality of the Father, we make the free choice, which he gave to us, harmful to ourselves instead of helpful toward salvation.[9] Let a certain holy ambition invade the mind, so that we may not be content with mean things but may aspire to the highest things and strive with all our forces to attain them: for if we will to, we can. Let us spurn earthly things; let us struggle toward the heavenly. Let us put in last place whatever is of the world; and let us fly beyond the chambers of the world to the chamber nearest the most lofty divinity. There, as the sacred mysteries reveal, the seraphim, cherubim, and thrones occupy the first places. Ignorant of how to yield to them and unable to endure the second places, let us compete with the angels in dignity and glory. When we have willed it, we shall be not at all below them.

But by what method? or by doing what? Let us see what they are doing, what life they are living. If we too live that life—for we can—we shall equal their lot. The seraph burns with the fire of charity; the cherub shines with the radiance of intelligence; the throne stands in steadfastness of judgment. Hence, if, dedicated to an active life, we undertake the care of lower things with a right weighing of them, we shall be made steadfast in the fixed firmness of the thrones. If, being tired of actions and meditating on the workman in the work, on the work in the workman, we are busy with the leisure of contemplation, we shall flash on every side with cherubic light. If by charity we, with his devouring fire, burn for the Workman alone, we shall suddenly burst into flame in the likeness of a seraph. Upon the throne, that is, upon the just judge, sits God, the judge of the

8 Psalms 48:21 (King James version, Psalms 49:20).
9 Psalms 81:6 (King James, 82:6), cf. John 10:34.

ages. He flies above the cherub, that is, the contemplator, and warms him, as if by brooding over him. The Spirit of the Lord is borne above the waters—I mean those waters which are above the heavens, the waters which in Job praise the Lord with hymns before daybreak.[10] He who is a seraph, that is, a lover, is in God; and more, God is in him, and God and he are one.

But in what way can anyone either judge or love things which are unknown? Moses loved God whom he saw, and as judge, he administered to the people what he formerly saw as contemplator on the mountain. Therefore with his own light the cherub in the middle makes us ready for the seraphic fire, and at the same time illuminates us for the judgment of the thrones. He is the bond of the first minds, the order of Pallas, the ruler over contemplative philosophy.[11] We must first rival him and embrace him and lay hold of him. Let us make ourselves one with him and be caught up to the heights of love. And let us descend to the duties of action, well instructed and prepared.

But if our life is to be shaped after the model of a cherub's life, it is well worth while to have in readiness and before our eyes what that life is and what sort it is, what actions and what works are theirs. Since we may not attain to this through ourselves, because we are flesh and our wisdom is of the earth, let us go to the ancient fathers who can give us a very substantial and sure faith in these things as things familiar and akin to them.[12] Let us consult the Apostle Paul, the vessel of election, because, when he was lifted up to the third heaven, he saw the armies of the cherubim in action. According to Dionysius' interpretation, he will answer that the cherubim are being purged, then are being illuminated, and lastly are being perfected.[13]

---

10 Compare Job 38:7, and Genesis 1:2.

11 Macrobius, *In Somnium Scipionis* I. 6. 11, 54-55.

12 Romans 8:5.

13 Pseudo-Dionysius, the Areopagite, *Caelestis hierarchia* VI-VII. The writings attributed to the unknown Dionysius, probably of the late 5th century A.D., contain a blend of Christian, Greek, and Jewish elements; they had an enormous influence on subsequent Christian theology.

Therefore, by rivaling the life of a cherub upon the earth, by confining the onslaughts of the affections by means of moral science, and by shaking off the mist of reason by means of dialectic, as if washing off the filth of ignorance and vice, let us purge the soul, that the affections may not audaciously run riot, nor an imprudent reason sometime rave. Then, over a soul which has been set in order and purified, let us pour the light of natural philosophy, that lastly we may perfect it with the knowledge of divine things.

And lest our Christians be insufficient for us, let us consult the patriarch Jacob, whose image flashes forth, carven in the seat of glory. That very wise father will give us advice by showing himself asleep in the lower world and awake in the upper. But his advice will be given figuratively: that is the way all things happen there. A ladder stretching from the lowness of earth to the heights of heaven and divided by the succession of many steps, with the Lord sitting at the top: the angels, contemplating, climb, by turns, up and down the steps.[14] But if we who are in pursuit of an angelic life must try to do this same thing, I ask, who can touch the ladder of the Lord with dirty feet or unwashed hands? As the mysteries put it, it is sacrilegious for the impure to touch that which is pure. But what are these feet, and what are these hands? Naturally, the feet of the soul are that most despicable portion which alone rests upon matter as upon the earth, I mean the nutritive and the food-taking power, kindling-wood of lust and teacher of voluptuous softness. As for the hands of the soul, we might as well have spoken of anger, which struggles as a defender for appetite and, like a robber under the dust and sunshine, carries off the things which will be squandered by the appetite, which is dozing away in the shade. But, so as not to be hurled back from the ladder as profane and unclean, let us wash these hands and these feet in moral philosophy as in living water—that is, the whole sensual part wherein the allurement of the body resides,

14 Genesis 28:12-13.

the allurement from which, they say, the soul gets a twisted neck, while being held back.[15] But, if we want to be the companions of the angels moving up and down Jacob's ladder, this will not be enough, unless we have first been well trained and well taught to move forward duly from rung to rung, never to turn aside from the main direction of the ladder, and to make sallies up and down. When we have attained that by means of the speaking or reasoning art, then, besouled by a cherub's spirit, philosophizing along the rungs of the ladder of nature, and penetrating through everything from center to center, we shall at one time be descending, tearing apart, like Osiris, the one into many by a titanic force; and we shall at another time be ascending and gathering into one the many, like the members of Osiris,[16] by an Apollonian force; until finally we come to rest in the bosom of the Father, who is at the top of the ladder, and are consumed by a theological happiness.

Let us inquire too of Job the just, what covenant he entered into with the God of life before he was begotten into life, the covenant which, among those million who stand before him, the highest God most strongly desired.[17] He will doubtlessly answer, Peace. Accordingly, since we read in Job that God makes peace in the highest,[18] and that the middle order interprets the prophecies of the highest order to the lower orders—let Empedocles the philosopher interpret for us the words of Job the theologian: he signifies to us that two natures are planted in our souls; by the one nature we are lifted upward to the heavens, and by the other, shoved downward to the lower world; and this by strife and friendship or by war and peace, according to his songs, in which he complains that, driven by strife and discord like a madman and banished from the gods, he is tossed upon the deep.[19] Indeed, fathers, there is multiple dis-

---

[15] *Asclepius* I. 12.

[16] Osiris, Egyptian god, was cut to pieces by Seth, and put together again by his wife, Isis.

[17] Daniel 7:10; cf. Jeremiah 1:5.

[18] Job 25:2.

[19] Empedocles, fr. 115 (Diels).

cord in us, and we have severe, intestine, and more than civil wars at home: if we are unwilling to have these wars, if we will strive for that peace which so lifts us up to the heights that we are made to stand among the exalted of the Lord, moral philosophy alone will still those wars in us, will bring calm successfully.[20] First, if our man will seek a truce with the enemy, he will subdue the uncurbed forays of the multiple brute, the quarrelings of the lion, and the feelings of wrath. Then if we take the right counsel, and desire for ourselves the security of everlasting peace, it will come and will fulfill our prayers liberally. The slaying of both beasts, like stuck sows, will establish most solemnly a most holy treaty between the flesh and the spirit. Dialectic will calm the turmoils of a reason shoved about between the fistfights of oratory and the deceits of the syllogism. Natural philosophy will calm the strifes and discords of opinion, which shake the unquiet soul up and down, pull her apart, and mangle her. But natural philosophy will bring calm in such a way as to command us to remember that, according to Heraclitus, our nature is born of war, and therefore is called a struggle by Homer; and hence, that in natural philosophy true quiet and lasting peace cannot offer themselves to us, and that this is the office and prerogative of their mistress, most holy theology.[21] Theology herself will show the way to that peace and be our companion and guide; and, as from afar she sees us hurrying, she will cry out, "Come unto me, ye that labor, and I will refresh you. Come unto me, and I will give unto you peace which the world and nature cannot give unto you!"[22] As we are called so sweetly and are invited with such kindness, let us fly on winged feet like earthly Mercuries into the embrace of our most blessed mother and enjoy the longed-for peace: the most holy peace, the indivisible bond, the friendship which is one soul, the friendship whereby all minds do not merely accord in one intellect that is above every intellect but in some inexpressible fashion become absolutely one. This is that friendship

20 Cf. Lucan, *Pharsalia* I. 1.
21 Heraclitus, fr. 53 (Walzer).
22 Matthew 11:28; John 14:27.

Soul married
to god

which the Pythagoreans say is the end of all philosophy. This is that peace which God makes on his heights and which the angels descending to earth announced to men of good will, that by this peace the men themselves ascending into heaven might become angels.[23] Let us desire this peace for our friends, for our age. Let us desire this peace for every house into which we enter. Let us desire it for our soul, that through this peace she may become the house of God; that after she has, through morals and dialectics, cast off her meanness and has adorned herself with manifold philosophy as with a princely garment, and has crowned with garlands of theology the summits of the gates, the King of Glory may descend, and, coming with the Father, may make his residence in her. If she shows herself worthy of such a great guest, as his mercy is great, then, in a golden gown as in a wedding dress, wrapped in a multiple variety of teachings, she will welcome her beautiful guest not as a guest but as a bridegroom. That she may never be divorced from him, she will long to be divorced from her own people and, forgetful of the house of her father, nay, forgetful of herself, she will long to die in herself that she may live in her bridegroom, in whose sight the death of his saints is surely precious —I mean death, if that should be called death which is the fullness of life, the meditation upon which the wise have said is the study of philosophy.[24]

Let us also cite Moses himself, scarcely inferior to the fountain fullness of holy and inexpressible intelligence, whence the angels are drunken on their own nectar. We shall hear the venerable judge promulgating laws to us who dwell in the desert solitude of this body: "Let those who are still unclean and in need of moral knowledge dwell with the people outside of the tabernacle in the open sky, and let them meanwhile purify themselves like Thessalian priests. Let those who have by now set their lives (mores) in order be received into the sanctuary. But let them not yet handle the sacred things; but first, as deacons assiduous in the service that is dialectic, let them

23 Jamblichus, *Vita Pythagoras* 230-233; Luke 2:14.
24 Plato, *Phaedo* 81.

minister to the sacred things of philosophy. Then, after they have been admitted to the sacred things, let them in the priesthood of philosophy contemplate sometimes the many-colored, that is, the star-constellated royal decoration of the higher palace of God, at other times the celestial candelabra divided by seven lights, and at other times the skin-covered elements, that finally they may be received through the merits of sublime theology into the sanctuary of the temple and may enjoy the glory of divinity without the veil of any image coming in between."[25] Moses gives us these direct commands, and in giving them he advises us, arouses us, urges us to make ready our way through philosophy to future celestial glory, while we can.

But in truth, not only the Mosaic or Christian mysteries but also the theology of the ancients show the advantages for us and the dignity of these liberal arts about which I have come here to dispute. For what else is meant by the degrees of initiation that are customary in the secret rites of the Greeks? First, to those who had been purified by moral and dialectic arts, which we have called, as it were, purgative, befell the reception of the mysteries. And what else can this reception be but the interpretation of more hidden nature by means of philosophy? Then lastly, to those who had been thus prepared, came that ἐποπτεία, that is, a vision of divine things by means of the light of theology. Who does not seek to be initiated into such rites? Who does not set all human things at a lower value and, contemning the goods of fortune and neglecting the body, does not desire, while still continuing on earth, to become the drinking-companion of the gods; and, drunken with the nectar of eternity, to bestow the gift of immortality upon the mortal animal? Who does not wish to have breathed into him the Socratic frenzies sung by Plato in the *Phaedrus,* that by the oarlike movement of wings and feet he may quickly escape from here, that is, from this world where he is laid down as in an evil place, and be carried in speediest flight to the heavenly Jerusalem.[1] We shall be possessed, fathers, we shall be possessed by these Socratic

25 Cf. Exodus 25-26.
1 Plato, *Phaedrus* 244 ff.

frenzies, which will so place us outside of our minds that they will place our mind and ourselves in God. We shall be possessed by them if we have first done what is in us to do. For if through morality the forces of the passions will have been so stretched to the [proper] measure, through due proportions, that they sound together in fixed concord, and if through dialectic, reason will have moved, keeping time in her forward march, then, aroused by the frenzy of the muses, we shall drink in the heavenly harmony of our ears. Then Bacchus the leader of the muses, in his own mysteries, that is, in the visible signs of nature, will show the invisible things of God to us as we philosophize, and will make us drunk with the abundance of the house of God. In this house, if we are faithful like Moses, holiest theology will approach, and will inspire us with a twofold frenzy. We, raised up into the loftiest watchtower of theology, from which, measuring with indivisible eternity the things that are, will be, and shall have been, and looking at their primeval beauty, shall be prophets of Phoebus, his winged lovers, and finally, aroused with ineffable charity as with fire, placed outside of ourselves like burning Seraphim, filled with divinity, we shall now not be ourselves, but He himself who made us.

The sacred names of Apollo, if anyone examines their meanings and hidden mysteries, will sufficiently show that that god is no less philosopher than prophet. Since Ammonius has followed this up sufficiently,[2] there is no reason why I should handle it in another way. But there come to mind, fathers, three Delphic precepts, very necessary for those who are to enter into the sacrosanct and very august temple of the true, not the invented Apollo, who illuminates every soul coming into this world. You will see that they give us no other advice than to embrace with all our strength this three-fold philosophy which the present disputation is about. For that μηδὲν ἄγαν, that is, nothing too much, rightly prescribes the measure and rule of all virtues through the principle of moderation, with which morals is concerned. Then that γνῶθι σεαυτόν, that is, know thyself, arouses us and urges us towards the knowledge of all nature, of

2 Plutarch, *De El Delphico* 2, 385b, in *Moralia.*

which man's nature is the medium and, as it were, the union.
For he who knows himself, knows all things in himself, as first
Zoroaster, and then Plato wrote in the *Alcibiades*.[3] At last,
illuminated by this knowledge through natural philosophy,
now near to God, saying εἶ, that is, Thou art, we shall address the
true Apollo with a theological greeting, familiarly and so happily.

Let us also consult the very wise Pythagoras, who was wise
especially in that he never thought himself worthy of the name
of wise. First, he will warn us not to sit too much, that is, not to
let go the rational part, by which the soul measures, judges, and
examines everything, and relax in idle inactivity. But let us
direct it diligently and arouse it by dialectical exercise and rule.
Then he will signify that we are to pay special attention to two
things, not to make water against the sun nor trim our nails
during the sacrifices. But after we have, through morals, relieved
ourselves of the appetite for overflowing sensual pleasures and,
as it were, trimmed the tips of our nails, the sharp pricks of
anger and the stings of animosity, only then may we begin to
take part in the aforementioned sacred mysteries of Bacchus,
and to be at leisure for our contemplation, whose father and
leader is rightly said to be the Sun. At last, he will advise us
to feed the cock, that is, to nourish the divine part of our soul
with knowledge of divine things as with solid food and heavenly
ambrosia.[4] This is the cock at the sight of which the lion, that
is, every earthly power, feels fear and awe. This is that cock to
which intelligence was given, as we read in Job.[5] At the crowing
of this cock, erring man returns to his senses. In the morning
dawn this cock daily crows in harmony with the morning stars
praising God. Socrates at the point of death, when he hoped
to unite the divinity of his soul to the divinity of a greater
world, said that he owed this cock to Asclepius, that is, to the
physician of souls, now that he was placed beyond all danger
of sickness.[6]

[3] Plato, *Alcibiades I*, 132c.
[4] Porphyry, *Vita Pythagoras* 42; Jamblichus, *Protrepticus* 21.
[5] Job 38:36.
[6] Plato, *Phaedo* 118a. Asclepius, or Aesculapius, the god of medicine.

Let us also examine the records of the Chaldaeans. We shall see, if we can believe them, that through these same arts, the way to happiness is opened to men. The Chaldaean interpreters write that it was a saying of Zoroaster that the soul has wings; when the feathers fall off, she is borne headlong into the body, when they sprout again, she flies up to the heights.[7] When his students asked him how they might obtain souls flying with well feathered wings, he said "You moisten the wings with the waters of life." When they again questioned him where they might seek these waters, he answered them figuratively (as was the custom of the man), "The paradise of God is washed and watered by four rivers. From the same place you may draw healthful waters for yourselves. The name of the river from the north is Pischon, which means straight, that from the west is Dichon, which signifies atonement, that from the east is Chiddekel, which means light, that from the south is Perath, which we can translate as piety."[8] Give close attention, fathers, and consider carefully that these doctrines of Zoroaster really mean nothing else than that by moral science, as by western waters, we may wash dirt from our eyes; by dialectic, as by a ruler pointing north, we may direct our eyesight along a straight line. Then, let us accustom our eyes in natural contemplation to bear the still weak light of truth, the beginning of the rising sun, as it were, so that finally by theological piety and the most sacred worship of God, we may, like the eagles of heaven, endure bravely the very radiant brightness of the midday sun. These are perhaps those morning, noon, and evening knowledges sung first by David and explained more fully by Augustine.[9] This is that midday light, which, perpendicular, inflames the Seraphim, and at the same time illuminates the Cherubim. This is that land toward which old father Abraham was always setting out. This is that place where there is no room for un-

---

[7] Cf. Psellus and Pletho, *In Oracula Chaldaica* (Amsterdam, 1688), pp. 81 and 91.

[8] Cf. Genesis 2:10-14.

[9] Psalms 54:18 (King James, 55:17). Augustine, *De Genesi ad litteram* IV. 29-30.

clean spirits, as the doctrines of the Cabalists and Moors teach. And if it is right to make public, even enigmatically, something from more hidden mysteries, after the sudden fall of man from heaven has condemned our heads to dizziness, and, according to Jeremiah, death has entered through the windows and stricken liver and breast, let us call Raphael the heavenly physician to free us by morals and dialectic as by saving medicines.[10] When we are restored to good health, Gabriel, the strength of God, will now dwell in us. Leading us through the wonders of nature, and pointing out the virtue and power of God everywhere, he will finally hand us over to the high priest Michael, who will distinguish the veterans in the service of philosophy with the priesthood of theology, as with a crown of precious stones.

These are the reasons, most reverend fathers, that have not merely inspired me but compelled me to the study of philosophy. I was certainly not going to state them, except as a reply to those accustomed to condemning the study of philosophy in princes especially, or more generally, in men of ordinary fortune. Already (and this is the misfortune of our age) all this philosophizing makes for contempt and contumely rather than for honor and glory. This destructive and monstrous opinion that no one, or few, should philosophize, has much invaded the minds of almost everybody. As if it were absolutely nothing to have the causes of things, the ways of nature, the reason of the universe, the counsels of God, the mysteries of heaven and earth very certain before our eyes and hands, unless someone could derive some benefit from it or acquire profit for himself. It has already reached the point that now (what sorrow!) those only are considered wise who pursue the study of wisdom for the sake of money; so that one may see chaste Pallas, who stays among men by a gift of the gods, chased out, hooted, hissed; who loves and befriends her does not have her unless she, as it were prostituting herself and receiving a pittance for her deflowered virginity, bring back the ill-bought money to her lover's money-box. I say all these things not without great grief and indignation, not against the princes, but against the phil-

All must ponder

10 Jeremiah 9:21.

Ends and means, doing for wrong ends

osophers of this age, who believe and preach that there should
be no philosophizing because there is no money for philosophers, no prizes awarded them; as if they did not show by this
one word that they are not philosophers. Since their whole life
is set on money-making or ambition, they do not embrace the
knowledge of truth for itself. I shall give myself this credit and
shall not blush to praise myself in this respect, that I have never
philosophized for any reason other than for the sake of philosophizing, that I have neither hoped nor sought from my
studies, from my lucubrations, any other gain or profit than
cultivation of soul and knowledge of truth, always so greatly
desired by me. I have always been so desirous of this truth and
so much in love with it that, abandoning all care of public and
private affairs, I gave my whole self over to the leisure of contemplating, from which no disparaging of the envious, no curses
from the enemies of wisdom, have been able so far or will be
able later to frighten me away. Philosophy herself has taught
me to weigh things rather by my own conscience than by the
judgments of others, and to consider not so much whether I
should be badly spoken of as whether I myself should say or do
anything bad. In fact, I was not ignorant, most reverend fathers,
that this disputation of mine will be as pleasant and enjoyable
to all you who delight in good arts and have wished to honor
it with your most august presence, as it will be heavy and
burdensome to many others; and I know that there are some
who have condemned my undertaking before this, and who
condemn it now under many names. Thus there are usually
no fewer, not to say more, growlers who carry on well and in a
holy way against virtue, than there are who do so wickedly and
wrongly against vice.

There are some who do not approve of this whole class of
disputes and this practice of debating in public about letters,
asserting that it makes rather for the display of talent and learning than for acquiring knowledge. There are some who do not
disapprove of this type of exercise, but who do not approve of
it at all in my case, because I at my age, in only my twenty-
fourth year, have dared, in the most famous city, in the largest

assembly of the most learned men, in the apostolic senate, to propose a disputation on the sublime mysteries of Christian theology, on the loftiest questions of philosophy, on unknown teachings. Others who give me leave to dispute are unwilling to give me leave to dispute about nine hundred questions, saying in slander that the proposal was made as needlessly and ambitiously as it was beyond my powers. I should have immediately surrendered to their objections if the philosophy which I profess had so taught me; and now, at her teaching me, I would not answer if I believed this disputation among us were set up for brawling and quarreling. Consequently, let every intent of detraction and irritation depart, and let malice, which, Plato writes, is always absent from the divine chorus, also depart from our minds.[11] And let us learn in friendly fashion whether I ought to dispute, and on so many questions.

First, to those who slander this practice of disputing publicly, I am not going to say much, except that this crime, if they judge it a crime, is the joint work not only of all you very excellent doctors—who have often discharged this office not without very great praise and glory—but also of Plato and Aristotle and the most upright philosophers of every age, together with me. To them it was most certain that they had nothing better for reaching the knowledge of the truth which they sought than that they be very often in the exercise of disputing. As through gymnastics the forces of the body are strengthened, so doubtless in this, as it were, literary gymnasium, the forces of the soul become much stronger and more vigorous. I would not believe that the poets signified anything else to us by the celebrated arms of Pallas, or the Hebrews when they say *barzel*, iron, is the symbol of wise men, than that this sort of contest is very honorable, exceedingly necessary for gaining wisdom. Perhaps that is why the Chaldaeans, too, desire that at the birth of him who is to become a philosopher, Mars should behold Mercury with triangular aspect, as if to say that if you take away these encounters, these wars, then all philosophy will become drowsy and sleepy.

11 Plato, *Phaedrus* 247a. Cf. *Timaeus* 29e.

But to those who say that I am not equal to this business, the reason in my defense is more difficult. For if I say that I am equal to it, perhaps I shall seem liable to the charge of boastfulness and self-conceit; if I confess myself unequal, of audacity and imprudence. You see what difficulties I have fallen into, in what a position I am, where I cannot without blame make a promise about myself which I cannot then without blame fail to fulfill. Perhaps I could bring forward that saying of Job, that the spirit is in all,[12] and hear with Timothy, "Let no one scorn your young manhood."[13] But from my conscience I shall say this truly, that there is nothing great or singular in us. Though I do not deny that I am very studious and desirous of the good arts, nevertheless I do not take to myself or lay claim to the name of learned man. Wherefore I laid such a great burden on my shoulders not because I was unconscious of our infirmity, but because I knew that this sort of struggle, that is, literary, was peculiar in that here it is a gain to lose. Consequently, anyone very weak can and should not only not disparage them, but also seek them voluntarily, since the loser truly receives benefit and not injury from the winner, for through him the loser returns home richer, that is, more learned and readier for future fights. Inspired by this hope, I, weak soldier though I be, have not been afraid to challenge the bravest and strongest of all to such a heavy battle. Whether it was an act of boldness or not can in any case be judged more rightly from the outcome of the fight than from my age.

It remains in the third place for me to answer those who are offended by the numerous multitude of things proposed, as if this burden sat upon their shoulders, and as if it were not I alone who have to endure this toil, howsoever great. It is certainly unbecoming and peevish to wish to set limits to another's industry, and, as Cicero says, to desire mediocrity in a case where the greater is the better.[14] All in all, it was necessary for

12 Job 32:8. The Vulgate reads, "The spirit is in men," *hominibus;* Pico reads "in all," *omnibus.*

13 I Timothy 4:12.

14 *De finibus* I. 1.

me either to fail or to succeed in such great undertakings. If I
should succeed, I do not see why it is praiseworthy for me to
distinguish myself on ten questions, while it is thought blame-
worthy for me to have distinguished myself on nine hundred.
If I should fail, they will have grounds for accusing me, if they
hate me; for excusing me, if they love me. This is so because a
young man of modest talents and scanty learning who has failed
in such a serious and great matter will merit pardon rather
than accusation. Indeed, according to the poet, "If strength
fails, boldness will surely be glory: in great things it is enough
to have willed."[15] But if in our age many men, imitating Gorgias
the Leontine,[16] have been accustomed not without praise to
propose a disputation not merely on nine hundred questions
but on all questions about all arts, why am I not allowed to
dispute without blame on many questions indeed, but still on a
fixed and determinate number? But, they say, this is needless
and ambitious. Yet I contend that I did this not needlessly, but
of necessity. But if they should consider with me my reasons for
philosophizing, let them reluctantly confess that it is clearly
of necessity.

Those who have devoted themselves to any one of the schools
of philosophy, inclining for example to Thomas or Scotus, who
now are much followed, can bring their doctrine into danger in
the discussion of a few questions. But I have resolved not to
swear by anyone's word, that I may base myself on all teachers
of philosophy, examine all writings, recognize every school.
Wherefore, since I had to speak on all questions (lest, if as
defender of a personal doctrine, neglecting others, I should
seem to be hampered by it), even if few questions might be
raised about individual doctrines, there could not fail to be
very many that were brought forward simultaneously concerning all. Nor should anyone condemn in me that wherever the
tempest bears me, I am brought as a guest. [17] For it was a prac-

---

15 Propertius, *Elegies* II. 10. 5-6.

16 Gorgias, *c.* 485-375 B.C., Sophist who claimed to be able to answer any
question; character in Plato's *Gorgias*.

17 Horace, *Epistles* I. 1. 15.

tice of the ancients to study every school of writers, and if possible, to pass over no treatises unread; and especially those of Aristotle, who because of this was called by Plato ἀναγνώστης, that is, reader. And it indeed belongs to a narrow mind to have kept oneself within one Porch or Academy. Nor can anyone have selected rightly his own doctrine from all, unless he has first made himself familiar with all.

Further, in each school there is something notable that it does not have in common with the others. But let me now begin with ourselves, whom philosophy has at last reached. In John Scotus there is certain vigor and breadth. In Thomas, a solidity and equilibrium. In Aegidius, a terseness and precision. In Francis, a sharpness and pointedness. In old Albert, spaciousness and grandeur. In Henry, so it seems to me, there is always something sublime and venerable.[18] Among the Arabs, there is in Averroes a firmness and steadiness. In Avempace and in Alfarabi, something grave and well meditated. In Avicenna, something divine and Platonic.[19] Among the Greeks universally there is, especially, a certain brilliance and chasteness of philosophy. In Simplicius, richness and abundance. In Themistius, elegance and concision. In Alexander, steadfastness and learning. In Theophrastus, a serious working out of things. In Ammonius, a smoothness and pleasingness.[20] And if you turn to the Platon-

18 John Duns Scotus, 1266?-1308, Franciscan; St. Thomas Aquinas, 1225-1274, Dominican; Aegidius, or Giles of Rome, 1247?-1316; Francis of Mayrone, d. c. 1326, Franciscan follower of Duns Scotus; Albert the Great, or Albertus Magnus, c. 1200-1280, Dominican, teacher of St. Thomas; Henry of Ghent, d. 1293, Augustinian.

19 Averroes, Ibn Rushd, 1126-1198, chief representative of Arabic philosophy in Spain, known as "The Commentator" on Aristotle. Avempace, Ibn-ae Sa'igh, d. 1138, first outstanding Spanish representative of Aristotelian-Neoplantonic tradition, laid ground for Averroes. Alfarabi, c. 870-950, Moslem philosopher in central Asia, was taught the Neoplatonism and Aristotelianism of Christian Arabic philosophers; influenced most later Arabic philosophers. Avicenna, Ibn Sina, 980-1037, Persian physician and philosopher, of Aristotelian and Plotinian influence.

20 Simplicius, 6th century, and Themistius, 4th century, Greek commentators on Aristotle. Alexander of Aphrodisias, 2nd-century commentator on Aristotle and head of the Lyceum in Athens. Theophrastus, 4th-3rd cen-

ists, to go over a few of them: in Porphyry you will be pleased by an abundance of materials and a complex religion. In Jamblichus you will feel awe at a more hidden philosophy and at the mysteries of the barbarians. In Plotinus there is no one thing in particular for you to wonder at, for he offers himself to our wonder in every part; and while he speaks in a divine manner about divine things, and of human things in a manner far above man, with a learned indirectness of discourse, the sweating Platonists scarcely understand.[21] I pass over the more recent: Proclus, abounding in Asiatic fertility, and those who have flowed from him, Hermias, Damascius, Olympiodorus[22] and many others, in all of whom there always shines that τὸ θεῖον, that is, divine something, the peculiar emblem of the Platonists. Further, if there is a school which attacks truer doctrines and ridicules with calumny the good causes of thought, it strengthens rather than weakens truth, and as by motion it excites the flame rather than extinguishing it. Moved by this reasoning, I have wished to bring into view the things taught not merely according to one doctrine (as some would desire), but things taught according to every sort of doctrine, that by this comparison of very many sects and by the discussion of manifold philosophy, that radiance of truth which Plato mentions in his *Letters* might shine more clearly upon our minds, like the sun rising from the deep.[23] What good was it if only the philosophy of the Latins would be treated, namely, Thomas, Scotus, Aegidius, Francis, and Henry, without the Greek and Arab philosophers? All wisdom flowed from the barbarians to

---

tury B.C., follower of Aristotle and his successor as head of the Academy. Ammonius Saccas, 175-242, Alexandrian Neoplatonist, teacher of Origen and Plotinus.

21 Porphyry, 232-c. 305, Neoplatonist, devoted disciple of Plotinus. Jamblichus, c. 250-c. 325, follower of Porphyry. Plotinus, 205-269/70, the most outstanding of the Neoplatonists, whose *Enneads* had much influence on Pico.

22 Proclus, 5th-century, most important representative of late Neoplatonism. Hermias, disciple of Proclus. Damascius and Olympiodorus are 6th-century followers of Proclus.

23 Plato, *Epistle VII*, 341d.

the Greeks, and from the Greeks to us.[24] So our people, in their way of philosophizing, always thought it enough for them if they remained with foreign discoveries and cultivated foreign things. What good was it to treat of natural things with the Peripatetics, unless the academy of the Platonists was also summoned, whose doctrine on divine things has always been held very sacred among all philosophies (witness Augustine), and also has by me now, for the first time after many centuries (as I know, and may there be no envy at the word), been brought forward publicly to undergo the test of disputation.

What good was it to have dealt with the opinions of others in any number, if, as though coming to a banquet of the wise without contributing anything, we brought nothing which would be our own, given birth and perfected by our mind. Indeed it is ignoble, as Seneca says, to know only by way of commentary, and, as if the discoveries of the ancients had closed the road for our industry, as if the force of nature in us were exhausted, to give birth to nothing from ourselves, which, if it does not demonstrate truth, at least points to it as from a distance.[25] But if a farmer hates sterility in a field, and a husband in a wife, certainly a barren soul is hated by the divine mind woven into it and allied with it, the more a far nobler offspring is desired from it.

Consequently I was not content to have added, beside the common teachings, much on the ancient theology of Mercury Trismegistus,[26] much on the doctrines of the Chaldaeans and of Pythagoras, and much on the more secret mysteries of the Jews, and I also proposed for disputation very many things discovered and thought out by us on natural and divine matters.

First, I have proposed the concord of Plato and Aristotle, believed by many before now, but adequately proved by no one. Among the Latins, Boethius, who promised to prove it, is not

24 Cf. Eusebius, *Praeparatio evangelica* X. 10. 2; XIV. 10. 43 ff. Theodoretus, *Curatio* I. 41e ff.

25 Seneca, *Epistles* XXXIII. 7.

26 Hermes Trismegistus, or the Egyptian god Thoth, reputed author of writings on occultism and theology of the first three centuries A.D.

found ever to have done what he always wished to do.[27] Among
the Greeks, Simplicius made the same declaration: would that
he had fulfilled his promise.[28] Augustine too wrote in his
Academica that there have been many who have attempted to
prove the same thing in their very subtle disputations, namely,
that the philosophy of Plato and of Aristotle is the same.[29]
Again, John the Grammarian,[30] although he says that Plato
seems to differ from Aristotle only to those who do not understand what Plato says, nevertheless left no proof of this to posterity. Further, we have added several points where the
thoughts of Scotus and Thomas, of Averroes and Avicenna,
which are considered to be discordant, we have maintained to
be in concord.

Second, we have put down the seventy-two new physical and
metaphysical doctrines which we have thought out in Aristotelian and Platonic philosophy. If one holds to them he will
be able, unless I am wrong, as will soon be clear to me, to solve
any question proposed about the things of nature or of God,
in a fashion far other than we are taught by that philosophy
which is read in the schools and cultivated by the doctors of
these times. And, fathers, no one should wonder that in my
early years, at a tender age at which it has been hardly permitted me (as some maintain) to read the meditations of others,
I should wish to bring forward a new philosophy. They should
either praise this philosophy if it is defended, or condemn it if
it is refuted; and finally, since they are to judge of these our
discoveries and our learning, they should reckon up not the
years of the author, but rather the merits or demerits of these
things.

Besides this we have brought forward something else new,
the ancient system of philosophizing through numbers. It was
held to by the early theologians, by Pythagoras in particular, by

---

[27] Boethius (5th-6th century), *De interpretatione* II. 3.

[28] Simplicius, *Categoriae* 28; *Physica* 404. 16.

[29] Augustine, *Contra academicos* III. 42.

[30] John Grammaticus or Philoponos, 7th-century Alexandrian commentator on Aristotle.

Aglaophamus, by Philolaus, by Plato and the early Platonists.[1] But in this age, this doctrine, like other famous ones, has so passed out of use by the negligence of posterity, that scarcely any traces of it are to be found. Plato writes in the *Epinomis*[2] that among all liberal arts and theoretical sciences the science of numbering is chief and most divine. Again, asking why man is the wisest animal, he answers that it is because he knows how to number. Aristotle also records this opinion in his *Problemata*.[3] Abumasar writes that there was a saying of Avenzoar the Babylonian that he who knows how to number knows all things. These things could not in any way be true if they had understood by the art of numbering that art at which now the merchants are expert above all. Plato also witnesses this, warning us in a loud voice not to confuse this divine arithmetic with mercantile arithmetic. Therefore, when, after many lucubrations, it seemed to me that I had explored that arithmetic which is so praised, I went to put this thing to a test, and I promised I would answer publicly, in order, to the seventy-four questions that are thought to be among the principal questions on nature and God.

I have proposed theorems about magic, too, wherein I have signified that magic is twofold. The first sort is put together by the work and authorship of demons, and is a thing, as God is true, execrable and monstrous. The other sort is, when well explored, nothing but the absolute consummation of the philosophy of nature. When the Greeks mention these, they call the first sort γοητείαν, not dignifying it in any way by the name magic. They call the second sort by its proper and peculiar name, μαγείαν, the perfect and highest wisdom, as it were. Porphyry says that in the language of the Persians, magician means the same thing as interpreter and lover of divine things means in our language.[4] Now there is a great, or rather, fathers, there is the greatest disparity and unlikeness between these arts. Not only the Christian religion, but all laws, every well ordered

---

[1] Proclus, *Commentary on Timaeus* V, Proem; *Theologia platonica* I. 6.
[2] Plato, *Epinomis* 677 ff.; *Republic* 525d-e.
[3] Aristotle, *Problems* XXX. 6, 956a.
[4] Porphyry, *De abstinentia* IV. 16.

state, condemns and curses the first. All wise men, all nations studious of things heavenly and divine, approve and embrace the second. The first is the most fraudulent of arts, the second is firm, faithful, and solid. Whoever cultivated the first always dissimulated it, because it would be in ignominy and disgrace of the author. From the second comes the highest splendor and glory of letters, desired in ancient times and almost always since then. No man who was a philosopher and desirous of learning good arts has ever been studious of the first. Pythagoras, Empedocles, Democritus, Plato, traveled across seas to learn the second. When they came back, they preached it and held it chief among their esoteric doctrines.[5] The first can be proved by no arguments nor certain founders; the second, honored as it were by most illustrious parents, has two principal founders: Xalmosis, whom Abbaris the Hyperborean imitated, and Zoroaster, not the one whom you perhaps think, but the son of Oromasus. If we question Plato as to what is the magic of each of them, he will answer in the *Alcibiades* that Zoroaster's magic is nothing but that knowledge of divine things wherein the kings of Persia educated their sons, that after the pattern of the republic of the world they might themselves be taught to rule their own republic.[6] He will reply in the *Charmides* that the magic of Xalmosis is medicine of the soul, by which temperance is obtained for the soul, as health is obtained for the body by medicine.[7] Afterwards Carondas, Damigeron, Apollonius, Hostanes, and Dardanus continued in their footsteps.[8] So did Homer, whom we shall prove sometime in our *Poetic Theology* to have disguised this magic too, just as he did all other wisdoms, under the wanderings of Ulysses.[9] Eudoxus and Hermippus continued in their footsteps.[10] Nearly all who have

[5] Pliny, *Natural History* XXX. 1 (2).

[6] Plato, *Alcibiades I*, 121 ff. Xalmosis or Zalmoxis, 6th century B.C., slave who later became a disciple of Pythagoras.

[7] Plato, *Charmides* 156.

[8] Cf. Tertullian, *De anima* 57.

[9] Pliny, *Natural History* XXX. 1 (2).

[10] *Ibid.* Eudoxus of Cnidus, c. 408-355, mathematician, astronomer, philosopher; studied under Plato. Hermippus, 5th century B.C., opponent of Pericles.

examined closely the Pythagorean and Platonic mysteries have continued also. I find three among the moderns who have caught the scent of it, Alchindus the Arab, Roger Bacon, and William of Paris [of Auvergne]. Plotinus too mentions it, where he shows that the magician is the minister and not the maker of nature.[11] That most wise man proves and asserts this second magic, so abhorring the other that, invited to the rites of evil demons, he replied that it was more fitting for them to come to him than for him to go to them, and rightly so.[12] For as the first magic makes man subject to and delivered over to the powers of wickedness, so the second makes him their prince and lord. Finally, the first cannot claim for itself the name of either art or science. The second is full of the deepest mysteries and includes the most profound and hidden contemplation of things, and finally, the knowledge of all nature. The second, among the virtues sown by the kindness of God and planted in the world, as if calling them out from darkness into light, does not so much make wonders as carefully serve nature which makes them. Having carefully investigated the harmony of the universe, which the Greeks very expressively call συμπάθειαν,[13] and having looked closely into the knowledge that natures have of each other, this second magic, applying to each thing its innate charms, which are called by magicians ἴυγγες,[14] as if it were itself the maker, discloses in public the wonders lying hidden in the recesses of the world, in the bosom of nature, in the storerooms and secrets of God. And as the farmer marries elm to vine, so the magician marries earth to heaven, that is, lower things to the qualities and virtues of higher things. Hence the first magic appears as monstrous and harmful as the second, divine and salutary. And especially because the first magic

[11] Alchindus or Al-Kindi, d. 873, the founder of Arab philosophy, an Aristotelian influenced by Neoplatonism. Roger Bacon, c. 1214-1292, English Franciscan. William of Auvergne, c. 1180-1249, Bishop of Paris. Plotinus, *Enneads* IV. 4. 42-43.

[12] Porphyry, *Vita Plotini* X. 34-35.

[13] "Sympathy." Pliny, *Natural History* XX. 1.

[14] *Scholia in Theocritum vetera* II. 17 (Wendel). Cf. *Oracula Chaldaica*, ed. Kroll, pp. 39 ff.; Psellus, *Hypotyposis* (ed. Kroll, 4, p. 73).

delivers man over to the enemies of God, calls him away from God, this second magic arouses that admiration at the works of God which so prepares that charity, faith, and hope most surely follow. For nothing impels more toward religion and the worship of God than assiduous contemplation of the wonders of God. When we shall have well explored these wonders by means of this natural magic we are speaking of, we shall be inspired more ardently to the worship and love of the maker, and shall be driven to sing: "The heavens are full, all the earth is full of the majesty of Thy glory."[15]

And this is enough about magic, about which I have said these things because I know there are many people who, as dogs always bark at strangers, so also often condemn and hate what they do not understand.

I come now to those things that I have dug up from the ancient mysteries of the Hebrews and have brought forward in order to confirm the holy and Catholic faith. And lest by chance they be thought by those to whom they are unknown to be fictitious nonsense or tales about rumors, I wish everyone to understand what and of what sort they are, whence sought, by which and how famous authors they are guaranteed, and how they were stored away, how divinely inspired they are, and how necessary to us for defending religion against the rude slanders of the Hebrews. Not only do celebrated doctors of the Hebrews, but also among us Esdras, Hilary, and Origen[16] write that Moses on the mountain received from God not only the law, which, as written down in five books, he left to posterity, but also a more secret and true interpretation of the law. But God commanded him to publish the law indeed to the people, yet not to pass on in writing the interpretation of the law, or to make it generally known, but to reveal it himself under a great holy seal of silence to Jesus Nave alone, and afterwards he to the other high priests

---

15 Isaiah 6:3.

16 Esdras or Ezra, Jewish priest and scribe active after return from his exile, 538 B.C. St. Hilary, Bishop of Poitiers, c. 300-367, wrote against Arian heresy. Origen, c. 185-c. 254, with exception of Augustine, the most influential theologian of the ancient church, much admired by Pico.

succeeding him.[17] It was enough to recognize by means of the plain story, now the power of God, now his anger against the wicked, his mercy toward the good, and his justice toward all; and by means of the divine and saving precepts to be taught to live well and blessedly, and the worship of the true religion. But to disclose to the people the more secret mysteries, things hidden under the bark of the law and the rough covering of words, the secrets of the highest divinity, what was that other than to give what is holy to dogs and to cast pearls among swine?[18] Consequently it was not human prudence but divine command to keep these things secret from the people, and to communicate them to the perfect, among whom alone Paul says that he spoke wisdom.[19] The ancient philosophers observed this custom very faithfully. Pythagoras wrote nothing but a few little things which, on dying, he entrusted to his daughter Dama. The sphinxes carved on the temples of the Egyptians warned them to guard mystical doctrines inviolate from the profane multitude, in the entanglements of enigmas. Plato, writing to Dionysius some things about the highest substances, says, "I must speak in enigmas, so that if the letter by chance comes into the hands of others, what I have written you may not be understood by them."[20] Aristotle said that his books of *Metaphysics,* which treat of divine things, are published and not published. What more? Origen asserts that Jesus Christ the master of life revealed many things to his disciples which they did not want to write down, lest they become common to the vulgar. Dionysius the Areopagite especially confirms this, who says that the more secret mysteries were handed down by the founders of our religion ἐκ νοῦ εἰς νοῦν διὰ μέσον λόγον, from soul to soul, without writing, by means of words passing down. Because that divinely given, true interpretation of the law of Moses was revealed by command of God in just this same way, it is called Cabala, which means the same thing among the Hebrews as *reception*

---

17 IV Esdras 14:45-47.
18 Matthew 7:6.
19 I Corinthians 2:6.
20 Plato, *Epistle II*, 312d-e. Jamblichus, *Vita Pythagoras* XXVIII. 146.

does among us. This is so because one man would receive this doctrine from another not through written records, but by regular succession of disclosure, by law of inheritance, as it were. But after the Hebrews had been liberated by Cyrus from captivity in Babylon, and the temple had been restored under Zorobabel, they turned their minds to repairing the law. Esdras, then governor of the church, after he corrected the book of Moses, clearly knew that the custom instituted by the forefathers of passing the doctrine on by hand could not be preserved through the exiles, slaughters, flights, and captivity of the people of Israel, and that the secrets of heavenly doctrine, granted to him by God, would henceforth perish, as they could not remain long in memory without the mediation of writings. Consequently, he decreed that all the wise men who were then left should be called together, and each of them should bring together what he remembered about the mysteries of the law. After scribes were summoned, it should then be written down in seventy volumes, for there were about that many wise men in the Sanhedrin. Do not take my word only for this, fathers, but listen to Esdras himself speaking, thus: "When forty days had passed, the most high spoke, saying: 'Place in the open what you formerly wrote, so that the worthy and unworthy may read. But you will save the last seventy books so that you may pass them on to the wise among your people. For in them is the heart of understanding and the fountain of wisdom and the river of knowledge.' And so I have done."[21] These are the words of Esdras. These are the books of the knowledge of Cabala. Esdras proclaimed at the beginning in a clear voice that in these books was rightly the heart of understanding, that is, an ineffable theology of supersubstantial deity, the fountain of wisdom, that is, an exact metaphysics of intelligible angels and forms, and the river of knowledge, that is, a most sure philosophy of natural things.

Pope Sixtus IV, who preceded Innocent VIII under whom we happily live, provided with the greatest care and zeal that

21 IV Esdra 14:45-47.

these books should be translated into Latin for the public advantage of our faith. And so, when he died, three of them came through to the Latins. In this age these books are cherished among the Hebrews with such religious awe that no one is allowed to touch them unless he is forty years old.

When I had procured myself these books at no small expense and had read them through with the greatest diligence and unwearied labor, I saw in them (God is my witness) a religion not so much Mosaic as Christian. There is the mystery of the Trinity, there the incarnation of the Word, there the divinity of the Messiah; there I read the same things on original sin, on Christ's atonement for it, on the heavenly Jerusalem, on the fall of demons, on the orders of angels, on purgatory, on the punishments of hell, which we daily read in Paul and Dionysius, in Jerome and Augustine. In those matters that regard philosophy, you may really hear Pythagoras and Plato, whose doctrines are so akin to Christian faith that our Augustine gives great thanks to God that the books of the Platonists came into his hands. In short, there is hardly any dispute between us and the Hebrews on this wherein they cannot be so disproved and refuted from the books of the Cabalists that there is no corner left in which they may hide. I have Antonius Cronicus, a most learned man, as a very trustworthy witness to this. When I was at his house at a banquet he heard with his own ears Dactylus the Hebrew, who was learned in this science, come down on his feet and hands to the exact belief of Christians on the Trinity.

But to return to the review of the topics of my disputation, we have advanced our opinion on the interpretation of the poems of Orpheus[22] and Zoroaster. Orpheus is read almost wholly in Greek, Zoroaster partly in Greek, but more completely in Chaldaean. Both are believed to be the fathers and founders of ancient wisdom. I am silent about Zoroaster, who is frequently mentioned by the Platonists, always with the greatest veneration. Jamblichus the Chalcidean writes that

[22] Orpheus, legendary founder of the religious, philosophical cult Orphism.

Pythagoras had the Orphic theology as the model after which he molded and formed his own philosophy.[23] In fact, they say that the words of Pythagoras are called holy only because they flowed from the teachings of Orpheus: thence as from their primal source flowed the secret doctrine of numbers, and whatever Greek philosophy had that was great and sublime. But, as was the practice of ancient theologians, Orpheus covered the mysteries of his doctrines with the wrappings of fables, and disguised them with a poetic garment, so that whoever reads his hymns may believe there is nothing underneath but tales and the purest nonsense. I wished to say this so that it may be known with what labor, with what difficulty I dug out the hidden meanings of a secret philosophy from the calculated meshes of riddles and from hiding-places in fables, especially with no help from the work and industry of other interpreters in such a weighty, abstruse, and unexplored field.

And still these dogs of mine bark that I have heaped up minutiae and trifles for a display of many questions, as if the questions were not all those which are doubtful and most controversial, with which the principal schools struggle; as if I did not advance many utterly unknown and untried questions to those very people who criticize mine and believe themselves the most eminent of philosophers.

I am so free from that guilt that I have taken care to reduce my disputation to as few headings as I could. If, as others usually do, I had wished to divide the disputation into its parts and cut it up fine, it would have expanded into a truly innumerable number. And, not to speak of the others, who is there who does not know that I could have spun out one of the nine hundred theses, that is, that the philosophies of Plato and Aristotle are to be reconciled, into six hundred headings, not to say more, beyond all suspicion of artificial multiplicity, enumerating one by one all the places wherein others think they disagree and I think they agree? But certainly (though I shall say something neither modest nor in accord with my character), I shall say, because the envious force me to speak,

[23] Jamblichus, *Vita Pythagoras* XXVIII. 145.

detractors force me, that I wished by this assembly of mine to show not that I know many things, but that I know things which many people do not know.

So that the fact itself may now be made evident to you, most venerable fathers, so that my discourse may no longer delay your desire, most excellent doctors, whom not without great delight I see ready and equipped, awaiting battle (may it be happy and fortunate), let us now, as by a trumpet summons, engage hands in combat.

On Being and the One

ON BEING AND THE ONE

to *Angelo Poliziano*[1]

Proem

You told me some days ago what Lorenzo dei Medici discussed with you concerning being and the one. Supported by the reasons of the Platonists, he disputed against Aristotle, on whose *Ethics* you are giving a public commentary this year. Lorenzo is a man of such powerful and multiform mind that he seems to be suited to everything. What I especially admire in him is his always speaking or meditating on some literary matter, even though he is always very occupied with the republic. And since those who think that Aristotle disagrees with Plato disagree with me, who make a concordant philosophy of both, you asked both how Aristotle might be defended in this matter and also how he might agree with his master, Plato. I said what came to my mind at that time, confirming what you answered to Lorenzo in the discussion rather than bringing in anything new. But this was not enough for you. Although I am to write at greater length on these topics in the *Concord of Plato and Aristotle* which I am now bringing forth, you entreated me to collect in a brief compendium what I said about this question then in your presence. Domenico Benivieni was by chance also present. He is very dear to us both, for his learning and for his honesty. What can I deny you? May I say that you are an almost inseparable companion, particularly in a literary matter? May I also be allowed, through you who vindicate a more elegant language, to use some words which are not yet perhaps legally given to Latin. Still, the newness of the subject makes such ex-

[1] Angelo Ambrogini (1454-1494), poet in Greek, Latin, Italian; intimate friend of Marsilio Ficino and Pico.

pression almost necessary, and therefore you should not look for the allurement of a more elegant style. As Manilius says, "The subject itself refuses to be ornamented; it is content to be taught."[2] If I remember correctly, these were the things that we discussed.

Chapter One

which tells the reasons of the Platonists, by which they maintain that the one is superior to being.

Aristotle says in many places that the one and being, and likewise the true and the good, correspond to each other and are the same in extent.[3] We shall treat of the true and the good later. The Academy opposes this, and thinks that the one is prior to being. When they say prior, they mean that the one is more simple and more universal. For this reason they also say that God, whose is the highest simplicity, is one, but not that he is being. They say that the prime matter of all things, rough and unformed, is within the limits of the one, but they maintain that it is outside the limits of being. Then they add that that which is opposed to the one is not the same as that which is opposed to being. That which is opposed to being is nothing, whereas that which is opposed to the one is multitude. Consequently, by the same rule by which those opposites are judged to be two, the Platonists think that being and the one are not convertible and do not correspond to each other.

Chapter Two

in which it is asked where Plato spoke of being and the one, and which shows that his words agree more with the view of those who say that the one and being are equal, than with those who wish the one to be superior to being.

[2] Manilius, *Astronomicon* III. 39.
[3] Aristotle, *Metaphysics* IV. 2, 1003 ff.; XI. 3, 1060b ff.

The latter use the following arguments. Before we refute them, it would be relevant to bring into central place what Plato may be found to have said on this question. I find that Plato disputed concerning being and the one in two places, namely, in the *Parmenides* and the *Sophist*. The Academics contend that in both passages Plato places the one above being.

But I shall first say this about the *Parmenides*.[4] Nothing in the whole dialogue is positively asserted. If anything is asserted, still nothing is clearly found by which we may ascribe this sort of teaching to Plato. That book is certainly not to be included among his doctrinal works, since it is nothing but a dialectical exercise. The words themselves of the dialogue are so far from refuting our opinion that there are no more arbitrary and forced commentaries than those brought in by persons wishing to interpret the *Parmenides* of Plato in another sense. But let us omit all the commentators. Let us look at the construction of the dialogue, where it begins, to what it tends, what it promises, what it asserts.

The dialogue is as follows. After disputing whether all things are one, or whether the things which are, are many, Socrates turned to the ideas, and asked Parmenides many questions concerning them. Parmenides replied to Socrates that he was pleased with his zeal and with his soul's desire to define the highest things. He said, "Consider, and while you are young, exercise yourself very diligently in that faculty which appears useless to many people, for which reason they call it trifling or garrulousness. Otherwise, truth may escape you."[5] All admit that Parmenides meant dialectic by these words. The following words make this evident. After this, when Socrates again asked Parmenides, "What sort of exercise is this, Parmenides?" Parmenides answered first that it was that sort that he had heard from Zeno. Then, Parmenides taught more particularly about this. He advised Socrates to examine with particular skill not only what would follow if some thing is, but also what would

4 Plato, *Parmenides* 127c-130a; 130b-135c-d.
5 Plato, *Parmenides* 135d (Pico here used the translation of Marsilio Ficino).

follow if it is not, then he should see what would follow that thing that we call being or not-being, as it refers to itself, or to others; and he would see what would follow other things, as they refer to themselves or to others. And when Parmenides had said many things on this topic, Socrates said: "You propose a difficult work, and I do not altogether understand you. But why do you not propose some hypothesis and examine it in the way in which you propose, in order that I may have a better understanding of it?" Parmenides answered that it would be laborious for an old man like himself. Then Zeno said that Parmenides should do it when he is in a gathering of few people; otherwise, he said, it would be unseemly for things of this sort to be examined by an old man in a multitude of persons, because few people know that such an examination and exercise is necessary for the attainment of truth.[6]

These words of Zeno entirely confirm what we have said. If we may believe Zeno, that of which Parmenides is to treat is such that it may not be examined by an old man openly in an assembly of many people. And if it is a question of divine orders, of the first principle of all things, as these Platonists wish to interpret it, what subject is more suitable to an old man or of what would he be less ashamed? But it is beyond all doubt, unless we should wish to deceive ourselves, that the matter to which Parmenides was about to turn was dialectic. Socrates had just asked him for it. Zeno, however, judged that it was the business of a young rather than of an old man. If we do not believe such witnesses, we may run through the dialogue, and we shall see that nowhere is anything affirmed, but everywhere it is merely asked: If some thing is, what would follow, and if some thing is not, what would then follow.[7] But the Academics have here taken the occasion of their opinion concerning being and the one from the fact that in the first hypothesis Plato discusses this problem in order that he may see what would follow if all things were one; and he replies that that one, which we suppose to be, will be indivisible, infinite, nowhere; and when Plato has enumerated many other attributes of this sort, he

---

6 Plato, *Parmenides* 136a-e.
7 Plato, *Parmenides* 137c-142b.

adds this also, among other things i.e., that that one will not be being.[8] Notice also (if this be not a dialectical exercise but conveys a doctrine concerning being and the one), how much these two differ, that is, to assert that the one is above being, and to assert this as future: that, if all things be one, then that one would not be being. Enough about the *Parmenides*.

In the *Sophist*, he says on this question that the one and being are equal rather than that the one is superior to being. I do not find where Plato explains that latter theory. The former view Plato signifies in many places, as through these words: "Now considering in this way, it is necessary that you admit that he who says something says some one thing." And then, "But he who does not say something necessarily does not say some one thing, that is, he says nothing."[9]

So much for Plato. Consequently, according to him, not-one and nothing are equals, indeed, they are the same. One and something are equals. After this, Plato proves further that not-being cannot be called one, and he concludes: "Being is not a characteristic of not-being: therefore the one is not a characteristic of not-being."[10] He speaks of the one that he previously said was equal to what is something. It appears, then, that Plato held it as certain that the one was being. But let this be so, let us grant that Plato affirmed something which he certainly nowhere affirmed. Well, let us examine in what sense Plato could have spoken truly, first laying down the foundations of the Aristotelean position in this way.

Chapter Three

which declares how being is understood by Aristotle, when he makes it equal to the one and embracing all things.

This term *being*, about which it is argued whether it be equal to the one, can be taken in two modes. The first is that when

---

8 Plato, *Parmenides* 137c-138b; 141d-142a.
9 Plato, *Sophist* 237d.
10 Plato, *Sophist* 238a-c.

we say *being,* we understand all that which is outside nothing. Aristotle employed the term in this way when he made being equal to the one. He did not adopt this way of speaking without a reason. As it is truly said, we ought to think as the few, and speak as the many. We think and believe for ourselves, we speak for others, that is, for the multitude, and therefore we speak so that we may be understood. The masses and the common people understand being in the following way. Being is all that to which existence is not lacking, and which cannot truly be called nothing. But we find that even those who are considered to be wisest among the very people who think the opposite have used the term *being* in this way. Parmenides the Pythagorean, when he said that that which is, is one, meant God, if we believe Simplicius and the many others who wish to defend Parmenides from those who calumniate him, as if he had said that all things are one.[11] His defenders reply with one voice that Parmenides never believed that there was no division, multitude, plurality in things. Parmenides himself openly admits there is, in other places in his poems. But, when he said that what is, is one, he meant that that to which the name of being truly belongs and which truly is, is one only. This one is God. Therefore, if we believe Parmenides and even his Platonic defenders, the one cannot be above being, unless it is above God. And that Parmenides denied that God is being is so far from the truth that he conceded the true name of being to God alone. Thus the solution of the first argument of the Platonists incidentally presents itself to us.

But also Dionysius the Areopagite, whom those who dispute against us make into a patron of their opinion, will not deny that God truly said to Moses "I am who am," which we read thus in Greek, ἐγώ εἰμι ὁ ὤν, that is, "I am being." [12] Rather, whenever they say that nothing or not-being is opposed to being as multitude is opposed to unity, they will concede necessarily that that which is not being is nothing or not-being, as that

11 Simplicius, *In Physicorum,* ed. Diehls, I, 147.

12 Pseudo-Dionysius, *De divinis nominibus* I. 6 (Migne, *Patrologia Graeca,* III, 596 AB). See above, n. 13, p. 8.

which is not one is many or a multitude. Consequently, if they
observe the same rule of speaking, they would have to say either
that God is nothing, which frightens the ears, or else that God
is being. When being is understood in this sense, we have established the first axiom and universal premise, that it is necessary to say about any thing either that it is or that it is not, but
that both at the same time can be either said or thought about
no thing. Therefore, since there is nothing outside all things
except nothing itself, if being, understood in this way, excludes
only nothing from itself, then without doubt being must include all things. For this reason the one cannot include more
things than being unless it includes nothing, which Plato
denies in the *Sophist,* when he says that not-being or nothing
cannot be called one. Nor does the one include fewer things
than being, as they themselves admit. Therefore, being and the
one are equals.

Chapter Four

which tells how something can be said to be superior to
being.

We have explained one of the two modes in which we said
that being could be understood. Those who use being in this
sense, as they can use it correctly, most truly affirm that nothing
is more universal than being. It remains for us to explain the
second sense of being, according to which it will be evident
that it is nevertheless also possible to say truly that there is
something which may be placed above the eminence of being.
  Some nouns are concrete, others abstract. Hot, shining, white,
man, are concrete. Heat, light, whiteness, humanity, are abstract. Their meaning and difference is that what is called abstract signifies that which is such from itself and not from
another. The concrete, on the other hand, signifies that which
is such not from itself, but by the gift of another. Thus, what is

luminous shines by light, what is white is white by whiteness, and man is man by humanity. Since nothing participates itself nor can the same determination be in the same thing both by itself and by participation from something else, it follows that what is called abstract cannot be named from the concrete. Consequently, it is not fittingly said that whiteness is white, that blackness is black; indeed, he who would say such things would be ridiculous, not because whiteness is black or heat cold, but because whiteness is so far removed from blackness, and heat from coldness, that whatever things are white are white by whiteness, and whatever things are hot, are hot by participation in heat. We deny that qualities are in a thing either because the thing does not have the qualities (as when we say that what is black is not white), or because the thing has the qualities in a more excellent way and in a more perfect nature than we signify it to have them with such a way of speaking. For example, we deny that whiteness is white, not because it is black, but because it is not-black not merely because it is white (which is the same as saying: since it has whiteness) but because it is whiteness itself. Let us turn to our subject. Being has the aspect of a concrete noun. *Being,* and *that which is,* are the same in meaning. This word *existence* [*esse*] seems to be the abstract form of the preceding terms. That which participates existence [*esse*] is called being [*ens*], just as that which participates light [*lux*] is called luminous [*lucens*], and that which has the act of seeing [*ipsum videre*] is called seeing [*videns*]. Therefore, if we should look at this exact signification of being, we shall deny being not only to what is not, and to what is nothing, but to that which is to such a degree that it is existence [*ipsum esse*], which is of itself and from itself, and by participation in which all things are. In the same way we shall deny hot not only to what is without heat, but also to what is heat itself. For God, who is the plentitude of all existence, is of this nature. He alone is of himself, and from him alone, with no interposing medium, all things proceed to existence.

For this reason, we may truly say that God is not being, but is above being, and that something is higher than being, that is,

God, and since the title one is given to God, we may consequently say that he is the one above being.

We also call God one, not so much expressing what he is, as the manner in which he is all things that he is, and the manner in which other things are from him. "The one is called God because he is all things in one," Dionysius says.[13] Again, "He is called one because he is the principle of all things which are, as unity is the principle of all numbers."[14] Consequently, if, as the Academics think, Plato affirms in the first hypothesis of the *Parmenides* that the one is higher than being, that one will be nothing other than God, as even the Academics admit. They assert by common consent that Plato there treats of the first principle of all things.[15]

But, someone may say, Aristotle will be in disagreement with Plato at least partially, because Aristotle never understood being in the sense that it be under the one, and that it not include God. Plato said both these things about the one. Those who say this have not read Aristotle. Aristotle too says this, and more clearly than Plato.

Aristotle says in *First Philosophy*, Book VI, that being is divided into being *per se* and accidental being.[16] Since being *per se* is in ten categories, there is no doubt among good interpreters that God is not included under this sort of being. God is neither accidental being nor is he contained under any of the ten genera into which being *per se* is divided. The Peripatetics universally divide being into substance and accident. Because of this, we understand being in a sense such that God is above being, and is not under being, as Thomas teaches in the *Commentaries on the Theological Sentences*, Book I.[17] I shall add that some Platonists glory without justification, as if they had a mystery which was unknown to Aristotle, when they say

[13] Pseudo-Dionysius, *De divinis nominibus* I. 7 (Migne, *P. G.*, III, 596 D).

[14] Pseudo-Dionysius, *De divinis nominibus* V. 6 (Migne, *P. G.*, III, 820 D-821 A).

[15] Plato, *Parmenides* 137c-142b-c.; Plotinus, *Enneads* V. 1. 8.

[16] Aristotle, *Metaphysics* VI. 2, 1026a ff.

[17] St. Thomas Aquinas, *In I Sententiarum*, d. 19, q. 4, a. 1.

that there are two proper names of God, one and good, and thus good and one are prior to being. For as we showed, the Peripatetics know how God can be understood as above being. We can also show that Aristotle gave especially these names, good and one, to God. In *First Philosophy,* Book XII,[18] after Aristotle has examined all being and separated minds, he asks finally (as turning after all things to the investigation of the properties of God alone) whether, in addition to the good which is in the universe of beings as in an army, there is any separated good, as in a leader of this army, and he decides that there is such a good, which good is God. Aristotle then proves in the same chapter the unity of God. In witness of this, after valid reasons, Aristotle also cites Homer: εἷς κοίρανος ἔστω, εἷς βασιλεύς.[19] Therefore, where is Aristotle in error, where does he differ from Plato? Where is he profane? Where has he an opinion about God less honorific than would be suitable?

Chapter Five

which states by what reason the Peripatetics ascribe many things to God which Platonists deny of him, and which teaches in what way we may ascend through four steps to the darkness which God inhabits.

Let us now refute the arguments of the Platonists by which they contend that the one is superior to being. They hold this, not in the sense in which we also agree with it, but in an absolute sense, against Aristotle. And although the first argument in which it was said that God is one, but not being, is sufficiently refuted from what has been said above, it would nevertheless be worth while to digress further, so that we may show why many things may be both truly affirmed and truly denied of

18 Cf. Aristotle, *Metaphysics* XII. 10, 1075a ff.

19 "Let there be one ruler, one king." Aristotle, *Metaphysics* XII. 10, 1076a; Homer, *Iliad* XVI. 204.

God, not only by different philosophers, such as Platonists and Peripatetics, but also often by the same author.

God is all things, and is all things most eminently and most perfectly. This would not be unless he so included the perfections of all things in himself that he excluded from himself whatever pertains to imperfection in things. We can, however, define under two heads whatever is imperfect in the things that are. One is when there is something in the thing which is less perfect within the genus of that thing. The other is when something is perfect in its genus, but is not thereby perfect absolutely, since it has only the perfection of one genus, and there are outside it many genera adorned with their perfections which are not included in the thing. An example of the first type of perfection is sensible knowledge. Sensible knowledge is not imperfect merely because it is only knowledge and not appetite, but because it is imperfect knowledge, not only because it requires a brute and corporeal organ, but also because it only attains the surface of things. It does not penetrate to the interior, that is, to the substance. That human knowledge which is called rational is, in turn, imperfect knowledge because it is vague, uncertain, shifting, and laborious. Add the intellectual knowledge of divine minds, which the theologians call angels. Even that is imperfect knowledge, at least because it seeks outside itself what it does not possess fully within itself, i.e., the light of truth which it lacks, and by which it is perfected. Take life. That life which is in plants, indeed that which is in every body, is imperfect not only because it is merely life, and not knowledge, but also because it is not pure life; rather, it is some vivification of the body, derived from soul, always flowing, always mixed with death, and thus is to be called death rather than life.[20] If perhaps you do not know, we begin to die when we first begin to live,[21] and death extends as long as life, and we first cease to die when we shall be separated from the body of this death through the death of the body. But the life of the

[20] Cf. St. Paul, I Corinthians 15:31; Romans 7:24.
[21] Cf. Seneca, *Epistles* CII; CXX.

angels is not perfect. Unless the vivifying ray of divine light constantly warmed it, it would all fall into nothingness. The same
is true of other things. Therefore, when you say that God is
knowing and living, notice first that the life and cognition
which are ascribed to him are understood as free from all these
imperfections, but this is not enough. There remains another
imperfection. Here is an example of it. Conceive a most perfect
life, that is, a life which is all life and pure life, having nothing
mortal, mixed with no death, which would require nothing outside itself in order to remain unmoved and to be permanent.
Conceive again a knowledge by which all things would be known
simultaneously and most perfectly. Add this, too, that the know-
er would know all these things in himself, so that he would not
seek truth which he would know outside himself, but he would
be truth itself. Still, both this life and this knowledge, although
each is most perfect in its genus, and is such that it cannot be
outside God, when so understood and distinct from each other,
are unworthy of God. God is infinite perfection of every sort,
but not merely in that he includes all such particular and infinite perfections in himself. In that case he would not be most
simple, nor would those things which are in him be infinite. He
would be one infinite compounded from many things infinite
in number but finite in perfection. To say or think this of God
is impious. If the life that is the most perfect life, but is only
life and not knowledge, and if in turn appetite or will that is
the most perfect will, but is still only will and is neither life nor
knowledge, and if other similar things be set in God, it is clear
that the divine life will be of finite perfection, since it would
have the perfection of life, but would not have the perfection of
knowledge and of appetite. Let us therefore remove from life
not only that which makes it imperfect life but also that which
makes it merely life, and likewise from knowledge and from the
other names we give to God; and then what shall be left over
from all these will necessarily be such as we wish God to be understood, that is, one, most perfect, infinite, most simple. Life
is a kind of being, and wisdom in turn is a kind of being, and
justice likewise; yet if you should take away the condition of

particularity and determination from these, what would remain
would not be this or that being, but being itself, being absolutely, being universal not by the universality of predication
but by the universality of perfection. Likewise, wisdom is a kind
of good, because it is this good that is wisdom and is not that
good that is justice. As Augustine says,[22] take away this, take
away that, that is, take away this particular limitation through
which wisdom is that good that is wisdom, which is not that
good that is justice. Likewise, justice has the goodness of justice
such that it would not have the good that is of wisdom. Then
you will see the face of God in an enigma, that is, every good
itself, good absolutely, the good that is the good of every good.
Thus as life is a being, it is also a one. It is one perfection, and
wisdom likewise is one perfection. Take away the particularity,
and there remains not this or that one, but the one itself and
the one absolutely. Therefore, as we said at first, since God is he
who is all things when all imperfection is removed, surely when
you have taken away from all things both the imperfection
which is under their genus and also the particularity of their
genus, what remains is God. Consequently, God is being itself,
the one itself, the good itself, and likewise truth itself.

We have now advanced two steps, ascending to the darkness
which God inhabits, purging from the divine names all blemish
that is from the imperfection of the thing signified. There now
remain two steps, of which one proves the deficiencies of names,
the other reveals the infirmity of our intelligence. These names,
being, true, one, good, mean something concrete, and, as it were,
participated. Hence we say that God is above being, above true,
above one, above good, since he is existence itself, truth itself,
unity itself, goodness itself. But we are still in light. God, however, has established his dwelling in darkness.[23] Therefore we
have not yet reached God. For until we also understand and
comprehend what we say about God, we are said to remain in
light, and what we say and feel about God is as inferior as the

22 Augustine, *Enarrationes in Psalmos* 134 (Migne, *Patrologia Latina*,
XXXVI, 1430-1474).
23 Psalms 17:12 (King James, 18:11).

Plato's 2.
Cave

capacity of our intellect is inferior to his infinite divinity. Let us rise to the fourth step and enter into the light of ignorance, and, blinded by the darkness of divine splendor let us cry out with the Prophet, "I have become weak in thy courts, O Lord,"[24] finally saying only this about God, that he is unintelligibly and ineffably above everything most perfect which we can either speak or conceive of him. Then we place God most eminently above even unity, goodness, truth, and existence, which we conceive. Dionysius the Areopagite saw this. After all that he wrote in the *Symbolic Theology,* in the *Theological Institutions,* in *On the Divine Names,* and in *On Mystical Theology,* he finally at the end of that work spoke as he could about God in a very holy way, as if he were already in the cloud. After some other things on the subject, he cried out: "He is not truth, nor kingdom, nor wisdom, nor one, nor unity, nor deity, nor goodness, nor spirit, so far as we can know him, nor does he have the name father or son nor any other of the things which are known to us or to anyone else in the world, nor is he any other of the things which are not nor any of the things which are, nor do the things which are know the divinity as it is, nor does it know the things which are as they are, nor is there any speaking of it, nor name nor science nor darkness nor light, nor error nor truth, neither is there any affirmation or negation of it."[25] That divine man said this.

Let us sum up what we have said. We shall see that we learn in the first step that God is not a body, as the Epicureans think, nor the form of a body, as they suppose who assert God is the soul of the heavens or of the universe, as the Egyptians thought, according to Plutarch and the Roman theologian Varro.[26] Both the Epicureans and the Egyptians derived strong support for idolatry from this, as we shall declare in another place. Even some of the Peripatetics are so stupid as to confirm that this is true and is the opinion of Aristotle. See how much these men

24 Psalms 83:3 (King James, 84:2).
25 Pseudo-Dionysius, *De mystica theologia* V (Migne, *P. G.,* III, 898-1046).
26 Plutarch, *De Iside et Osiride* 49; Varro (116-27 B.C.), *De lingua Latina* V. 10.

fall short of the true knowledge of God! They remain at the starting point as if they were at the goal. Then they believe that they have reached the heights of God when they are still lying on the ground and have not yet moved a step toward him. According to them, God would not be perfect life nor perfect being nor even perfect intellect. But we have attacked this opinion at length in the fifth decade of our *Concord.*

In the second step we learn what very few comprehend rightly and in which we can all the more err if we should deviate a little from true intellect. We learn that God is not life nor intellect nor intelligible, but rather something better and more excellent than all these. For all these names signify some particular perfection of which there is none in God. Observing this, Dionysius and then the Platonists deny that life and intellect and wisdom and things similar to these are in God. God himself, by his unique perfection, which is his infinity, his deity, which he himself is, unites and collects all the perfection of these things, which in them is many and divided. God does not unite these perfections as one from these many, but as one prior to these many. Consequently, some other thinkers, and especially the Peripatetics, whom the Parisian theologians follow in almost all matters as far as is allowed, grant that all these perfections are in God. When we say and believe this we not only say and believe rightly, but we do this in agreement with those who deny these perfections, if the doctrine of Aurelius Augustine is always before our eyes, that the wisdom of God is not more wisdom than justice, and the justice of God is not more justice than wisdom, and likewise life is not more life in him than knowledge, nor knowledge more knowledge than life.[27] All these are one in God, not through a confusion or mixing or as a mutual penetration of distinct things, but through simple, highest, ineffable, originative unity, in which every act, every form, every perfection is comprised as in the first highest leader in the innermost treasury of divine infinity. They are comprised excellently, above all things and outside all things, yet in such

---

[27] Augustine, *Sermon* 340, I, 5 (Migne, *P.L.,* XXXVIII, 1498).

a way that not only are they very profound in all things, but are more one with all things than they are with themselves. Words fail, and this is expressed even less than it is understood.

But see, my Angelo, what madness seizes us. While we are in the body we can love God more than we can speak of him or know him. In loving we profit more, we labor less, we obey him more. Yet we prefer to be always seeking him through knowledge and never finding what we seek, rather than to possess by loving that which would be found in vain without loving. But let us return to our topic. It now appears clearly to you how God sometimes may be called mind and intellect and life and wisdom, and on the other hand may sometimes be placed above all these. Both these views may truly be affirmed and in agreement with each other. Plato does not disagree with Aristotle when, in *Republic*, Book VI, he places God, whom he there calls the idea of the good, above intellect and intelligible things, giving knowledge to intellects and intelligibility to intelligible things.[28] Aristotle, however, often calls God both intellect and intelligent, and intelligible. Even Dionysius, although he says the same thing as Plato, also does not deny with Aristotle that God is not ignorant of himself and other things. Consequently, if he knows himself, he is intellect and intelligible, for necessarily he who knows himself both knows and is known. Still, as I have said, if we understand these perfections as individual, or if, when we say intellect, we signify the nature that tends outside itself to the intelligible as to another thing, then Aristotle, no less than the Platonists, will most steadily deny that God is also intellect and intelligible.

In the third step, the nearer we approach darkness the clearer it becomes to us that we should not only not imagine with impious thought that God is some imperfect and, as it were, deficient being, as he would be if he were said to be either body or the soul of a body, or an animal constituted from body and soul. Let us not make him by human wisdom some particular genus, even the most perfect genus. For example, we should not

---

28 Plato, *Republic* VI, 509b; Cf. Aristotle, *Metaphysics* XII. 7, 1072b.

call him life or mind or reason. But we should know that he is
better than even what universal names indicate, such as one,
true, being, and good.

In the fourth step we know that he is not only above such
perfections, but above every name that can be formed, above
every notion that can be conceived by us. Then for the first
time we know him in some way when we are altogether ignorant of him.

It can be concluded from this that God is not only that than
which no greater can be conceived, as Anselm said,[29] but he is
that which is infinitely greater than every thing that can be
thought, as David the prophet truly says according to the Hebrew text: "Silence is praise to you."[30]

Let us say that this is the solution of the first argument. It
also opens a great window of legitimate understanding upon
the books of Dionysius entitled *On Mystical Theology* and *On
the Divine Names*. In these books we must be careful not to
underestimate what he wrote, since it is sublime. Nor, when
we judge all that we understand to be little, should we invent
for ourselves dreams and inextricable fictions.

Chapter Six

which solves the second argument of the Platonists, on
prime matter.

The objection of the Platonists on prime matter is trifling.
Insofar as prime matter is being, it is one. If the followers of
Plato wish to follow him exactly, they must concede that prime
matter has less the character of one than of being. Plato did not
mean that prime matter was absolutely nothing. If that were
so, how could it be the receptacle of forms, a nurse, a nature,
and the other things that Plato says of it in the *Timaeus?*[1] Con-

29 St. Anselm, *Proslogium* XV (Migne *P.L.*, CLVIII, 235).
30 Psalms, reference uncertain. Pico interprets the Hebrew text.
1 Plato, *Timaeus* 49a; 51a; 52d.

sequently, it is not nothing, i.e., entirely without being, if we believe Plato who still in the *Philebus* calls matter not only multitude (which according to the Platonists is opposed to the one as nothing is opposed to being), but also calls it infinite.[2] But multitude, if it is finite, does not altogether escape the characteristics of the one, because what makes a multitude finite. makes it one. Thus an infinite multitude does not have the nature of the one, as it does not have the nature of limit. Therefore, prime matter, according to Plato, is more being than it is one. Those who deny this say that prime matter is not being, and yet they say that it is one, so that they may prove that the one is superior to being. Jamblichus the Platonist, in the book which he wrote, *On the Pythagorean Sect*, calls prime matter duality. This is because duality is the first multitude and is the root of all the other multitudes. Prime matter, according to him who is so great among Platonists as to be called divine, is not only not one but is a multitude, and is the root of all multitude that is in things. We have said these things to reply to them with his own arguments. Further, prime matter is neither altogether without unity nor without being. Prime matter receives its precise unity from the same form from which it receives being. I pass over the dispute concerning the affirmative or negative unity of prime matter, which is all very well known to those who have made even a slight acquaintance with Aristotle.

Chapter Seven

which solves the third argument of the Platonists, on multitude, and shows those who say that the one is more universal than being that something must be conceded that Plato denied.

They are greatly in error on this third argument. Multitude is not opposed to the one in the same way as not-being is opposed to being. Not-being is opposed to being as its contradictory,

2 Plato, *Philebus* 16c; 23c-27e.

whereas multitude is opposed to the one as its privation or contrary. Aristotle examines this at length in *First Philosophy, Book X.*[3] Those who are called Platonists see what disasters they fall into when they say that the one is above being. It is certain that when genera are so related that one is under the other as under a more universal genus, it may happen that something may be outside that which is included in the lower genus, and yet not be outside the higher genus. This is why the higher genus is called more universal. Here is an obvious example. Because animal is more universal than man, it can happen that something be not-man or not be man which is nevertheless an animal. For the same reason, therefore, if the one is more universal than being, it could happen that something be not-being or nothing which nevertheless would be one, and thus one would be predicated of not-being, which Plato expressly refutes in the *Sophist.*[4]

Chapter Eight

which declares how these four, being, one, true, and good, are in all things that are after God.

It is very truly said that these four, being, one, true, and good, include all things, if they are understood so that their negations are nothing, divided, false, and evil. Two others were added to these four, namely, something and thing, by later followers of Avicenna. Avicenna interpolated the philosophy of Aristotle in many places, and because of this, Avicenna had a great war with Averroes. But as regards this question, there is little disagreement.[5] These thinkers divide what is understood under one into one and something, which is not in disagreement with Plato, who in the *Sophist* enumerates something among these

[3] Aristotle, *Metaphysics* X. 3, 1054b.

[4] Plato, *Sophist* 238d.

[5] Avicenna, *Metaphysics* I. 4. Cf. Helias Cretensis, *Quaestio de ente, essentia et uno.*

most universal terms, and what is contained under being they divide into being and thing.[6] We shall discuss this elsewhere. Let us continue what we have begun. These four are other in God than what they are in the things that are after God, because God has them from himself, and other things have them from him.

Let us first see how they are in created things. All things that are after God have an efficient, exemplary, and final cause. All things are from him, through him, and to him. If, therefore, we consider things as they are constituted by God as efficient cause, they are called beings, because they participate being from God as efficient cause. If we consider things as they fit and correspond to their exemplar, which we call idea, according to which God established them, they are called true. An image of Hercules is called true when it corresponds to the true Hercules. Things are called good if they tend to God as to their last end. But if each thing be taken according to itself, absolutely, it is called one. There is this order. First, each thing is conceived under the concept of being, because the agent produces each thing before the thing is something in itself, otherwise the effect would not be from the cause according to all that it is. Consequently, there is nothing after God that we do not understand as being from another, finite being, participated being. One follows being. Truth is third, because after something is in itself, it must be seen whether it be like the exemplar according to which it was formed. If the thing is similar, it follows that it turns itself through goodness toward its exemplar as to the like and similar. Who does not see that these attributes are the same in extension? Give something being, and it is certainly also one. Who does not say one, says nothing, as Plato says in the *Sophist*. Whatever is, is undivided from itself and divided from other things which are not itself. We mean this when we say one, or, speaking with the words of Plato, "it is the same as itself and other than other things," which, Plato affirms in the same dialogue, is true of each thing. Every being is also necessarily true. If something is a man, then it is a true man, and it is the same

6 Plato, *Sophist* 251a-253b.

to say that a thing is not true gold, and to say that it is not gold. When you say, "It is not true gold," you mean this: "It seems to be gold and it is something like gold, but it is not gold." Consequently, Aurelius Augustine, defining what is true in the *Soliloquia*, says, "True is that which is."[7] This should not be understood as meaning that being and true are the same, for even though they are the same in fact, nevertheless in concept and definition they are different. Consequently, one ought not to be defined through the other. But Augustine wanted to say this: A thing is called true when it is what it is called and is said to be, as gold is true when it is gold and is not other than gold. Therefore this is what he said, "True is that which is." Those who do not notice this falsely attack the definition.

Likewise, any being is good because whatever is, insofar as it is, is good. Olympiodorus is much mistaken, in my opinion, in believing that he proves that good and being are other because we desire the good without qualification, but not being, only well-being.[8] Consequently it can happen that if we fare badly, we may desire not to be. Let us omit the question whether those who fare badly and are miserable can desire with a right and natural desire not to be. Olympiodorus does not notice that the good is multiple just as being is multiple.

In the first place, there is a natural being of things, as for a man to be man, for a lion to be lion, for a stone to be stone. Natural goodness undividedly follows this being.

There are other beings which can be called accidental, such as for a man to be wise, beautiful, healthy. Just as wisdom and beauty are different beings from humanity, even so they are different goods. Humanity, by which man is man, is a different good from wisdom, by which man becomes no longer man, but wise man. Thus humanity and wisdom both are and are called different beings.

Consequently, just as all things desire the good, even so all things desire being, and first of all they desire that goodness

[7] Augustine, *Soliloquia* II. 5 (Migne, *P.L.*, XXXII, 889).

[8] Olympiodorus (6th-century Neoplatonist), *In Phaedrum* 188, 29 (Norvin).

that follows upon natural being, since this goodness is the foundation of subsequent goodnesses, which are all added to it in such a way that without this goodness the others cannot be. How will he be happy who altogether is not? Indeed, that goodness that beings attain when they first are does not suffice for them. They desire to attain the other goods, which complete and adorn it. Just as we truly say that they desire other goodnesses besides the first goodness, even so we truly say that they desire other beings besides the first being, because to be happy is other than to be man. If anyone should grant that it can happen that someone does not wish to be unless he is happy, it would not follow, as Olympiodorus thought, that good and being were different, but that man is another being than happiness, and that the goodness of man is other than the goodness of happiness. Man desires the goodness of man only if he has the goodness of happiness too.

I omit the questions of whether something is called good absolutely and being absolutely for the same reason; of whether being is called good absolutely and good is called being absolutely; for this is not the place to discuss everything.

Consequently, we have said that each thing that is, is good insofar as it is. "For God saw all things which he made and they were very good."[9] Why not? They are from a good artisan, who impressed his likeness upon all things that are from him. Therefore, in the being of things, we can admire the power of God working; in truth, we can venerate the wisdom of the artisan; in goodness, we can love in return the liberality of the lover; in unity, we can receive the unique (as I may say) simplicity of the founder, who united each thing to itself, then all things to each other, then all things to himself, calling each thing to love of itself, of other things, and finally of God.

Let us also examine their opposites, whether they are likewise the same in extension. The reasons we have given above show that the false is the same as nothing. If we say that evil and nothing differ, the philosophers and theologians both will object, because to make evil is to make nothing, and it is cus-

9 Genesis 1:12.

tomarily said that there is no efficient, but only a deficient cause of evil. This refutes the insanity of those who posited two principles, one of goods, the other of evils, as if there were some efficient principle of evil. To divide a thing is the same as to destroy it, and thus we cannot take away from anything its own natural unity in such a way that its being would nevertheless remain in its integrity. The whole is not its parts, but that one thing which emerges from the parts, as Aristotle teaches in *First Philosophy*, Book VIII.[10] Thus if you divide the whole into parts, the parts remain, but the whole which is divided does not remain, but ceases to be in act and is only in potency, as parts which first were in potency then begin to be in act. The parts which were formerly in the whole did not have their own unity in act. This unity first appears when the parts, separated from the whole, subsist through themselves.

Chapter Nine

which declares how these four are in God.

Let us examine once more how these are in God. They are not in God in relation to a cause that God does not have; for he, the cause of all things, is from nothing. They can be considered in God in two ways, either as he consists absolutely in himself, or as he is the cause of other things. This distinction does not befit created things, as regards the present topic, since God is able not to be a cause, whereas other things are not able not to be from God. Therefore we conceive God first as the university of all act, the plenitude of existence.

It follows from this knowledge that God is one, therefore no opposite can be conceived. See how those who imagine many principles, many gods, are in error. It follows immediately that God is most true. What does he who is existence itself have which might appear to be and not be? It follows certainly that he is truth itself. He will also be goodness itself. There are three conditions of good, as Plato writes in the *Philebus*.[11] The

---

10 Aristotle, *Metaphysics* VIII. 3, 1044a25 ff.; VII. 6, 1045a7 ff.
11 Plato, *Philebus* 20c-d.

good is perfect, sufficient, and desirable. What we conceive in this way will be perfect because nothing will be lacking to him who is all things. He will be sufficient, because nothing will be lacking to those who possess him in whom they find all things. He will be desirable, because from him and in him are all things which for any reason can be desired. Therefore God is the fullest being, individual unity, most solid truth, most blessed good. If I am not mistaken, this is that τετρακτύς, that is, quaternity, by which Pythagoras swore and which he called the principle of ever-flowing nature. We have demonstrated that these things, which are one God, are the principles of all things. But we also swear by that which is holy, firm, divine; what is firmer, holier, or more divine than these things? If we were to assign these four names to God as he is the cause of things, the sequence must be reversed. First, he would be one, since he is understood in himself before he is understood as cause. Second, he would be good; third, true; fourth, being. Because the cause that is called the end is prior to the exemplary, and the exemplary cause prior to the efficient cause (for first we seek to have what may protect us from the harm of storms, then we conceive the idea of house in mind, finally we form the house outside by making it in matter), therefore, if, as we said in the preceding chapter, good pertains to the final cause, true to the exemplary cause, being to the efficient cause, then God, as he is cause, would have first the character of good, then of true, finally of being. We touch briefly on all these points, which are still full of many and great questions.

Chapter Ten

in which the whole argument turns to the ordering of life and the improvement of conduct.

Lest we dispute for others rather than for ourselves, we must be careful that while we are investigating the highest things we do not live in a low condition, that is, unworthy of those whom heaven has enabled to explore the reasons even of heavenly things. We must constantly remember that this our mind, to which even divine things are accessible, cannot be of mortal race, and will be happy only by the possession of divine things. Mind wanders here as a stranger, and approaches happiness insofar as it raises itself more and burns for divine things, having put aside concern with earthly things. The present disputation seems above all to warn us that if we wish to be blessed, we must imitate the most blessed of all things, God, possessing in ourselves unity, truth, and goodness.

Ambition disturbs the peace of unity and wrenches the soul that clings to it out of itself, and drags and tears the soul in pieces as if wounded. Who will not lose the splendor and light of truth in filth, in the darkness of pleasures? Raging greed, that is, avarice, steals goodness from us. It is characteristic of goodness to communicate to others the goods that it possesses. Consequently, when Plato asks why God created the world, he answers himself, "Because he was good."[12] These are those three, the pride of life, the lust of the flesh, and the lust of the eyes, as John writes, which are of the world and are not of the Father, who is unity itself, truth itself, goodness itself.[13] Let us therefore flee from here, that is, from the world which is established in evil; let us fly to the Father where there is unifying peace, truest light, best pleasure. But who will give us wings that we may fly higher?[14] The love of the things that are above.[15] Who will take this away? The desire of earthly things, which, if we follow it, will make us lose unity, truth, and goodness. We are not one if we do not bind, by the union of virtue, sense bent downward with reason which looks at heavenly things. If there are two princes in us, reigning in turns, as it were, we for a time follow God with the law of mind, for a time follow Baal with the law of the flesh, and our kingdom divided against itself is utterly desolated. If we are one in such a way that reason is en-

---

12 Plato, *Timaeus* 29e.
13 I John 2:16; I John 5:19.
14 Psalms 54:7 (King James, 55:6).
15 Colossians 3:1-2.

slaved by sense, and only the law of the members commands, this would be a false unity, since we would not be true. We would be called and appear to be men, that is, animals living by reason, and yet we would be brutes, for whom sensual desire is law. We would thus be deceiving those who see us, among whom we live. The image would not correspond to its exemplar. For we are the image of God. God is a spirit. We would not be spiritual, as Paul says, but animals.[16] When through truth we do not fall short of the exemplar, it follows that we who strive for the exemplar will finally be joined to it through goodness. If these three, one, true, and good, follow being by perpetual connection, it follows that when we are not these three, we absolutely are not, even though we may appear to be; and although we may be thought to live, yet we would be ever dying rather than living.

[16] I Corinthians 2:14; 15:46.

Heptaplus

Roberto Salviati

to Lorenzo dei Medici:

Greetings

Since, most illustrious Lorenzo, my nature and temperament are such as to make me love, cherish, and honor those who are either distinguished by their talents or remarkable for their learning, I have been unable to refrain from loving and admiring above all others your friend Pico della Mirandola, a man most worthy of all admiration. Since he recently dedicated to you a book, *The Sevenfold Narration of the Six Days of Genesis,* the first fruits of his studies, and a most distinguished work not only in my opinion but in the judgment of all, I determined to have it published in a correct edition at my expense, feeling sure that thus I would serve both my love for him and the general advantage of scholars. I hoped also to do something not unpleasing to you, if those natural and divine mysteries which he imparted to you should at last by me be made common to all men. Farewell.

Dedication by the publisher of the original edition of 1489.

THE HEPTAPLUS

ON THE SEVENFOLD NARRATION OF THE SIX DAYS OF GENESIS

To Lorenzo dei Medici

Proem

Emulation of your studies, Lorenzo dei Medici, has moved me to examine the secrets of the book of Moses, since last winter I noticed that in whatever leisure the state allowed you, there was nothing to which you applied yourself more assiduously or with greater pleasure than to the reading of them. A personal reason also has urged me to this: my other work, now long growing under your auspices and in your name, in which I have tried not only to free the Psalms of David, as translated by the Seventy Scholars[1] and still resounding in the church, from every doubtful reading and distortion, but also to illuminate them with the torches of interpretation. For this, I have found no treatise more useful or fruitful than these books, and none more suitable or (to speak truly) more necessary. During these days, moreover, it happened that I was continually concerned with the making of the world and with those celebrated works of the six days, in which there is great reason for us to believe that the secrets of all nature are contained.

To pass over the fact that our Prophet learned all these things through the inspiration of God and the dictation of the Holy Spirit, the master of all truth, has not the tradition not only of our own times but of his own race and of the gentiles reported him to us as most learned in human wisdom and in all

---

1 The Septuagint.

the fields of science and letters? There exists among the Hebrews, under the name of the wise Solomon, a book called
Wisdom, not the one we now have, the work of Philo, but another, written in that secret language called *Hierosolyma,* in
which the author, an interpreter, it is thought, of the nature
of things, confesses that he got all his learning of that sort from
the inner meaning of the Mosaic law.

We have the weighty authority, moreover, of both Luke and
Philo that Moses was deeply learned in all the lore of the
Egyptians.[2] All the Greeks who have been considered the most
excellent took the Egyptians as teachers: Pythagoras, Plato,
Empedocles and Democritus. The saying of the philosopher
Numenius that Plato was nothing but an Attic Moses is well
known.[3] The Pythagorean Hermippus attests that Pythagoras
copied many things from the Mosaic law into his own philosophy.[4] Therefore if in his books Moses seems an unpolished pop-
ularizer rather than a philosopher or theologian or master of
great wisdom, let us call to mind that it was a well-known practice of the sages of old either simply not to write on religious
subjects or to write of them under some other guise. For this
reason these subjects are called mysteries (and things which are
not secret are not mysteries); this has been observed by the Indians, by the Ethiopians, who took their name from their
nudity,[5] and by the Egyptians, and the sphinxes in front of the
temples hinted at this. Instructed by them, Pythagoras became
a master of silence, and he himself did not entrust anything to
writing except a very few things which, when dying, he left to
his daughter Dama. Those golden verses that are circulated are
not by Pythagoras, as is commonly believed even by the more
learned, but by Philolaus.[6] The Pythagoreans, one after an-

[2] Acts 7:22.

[3] Fr. 13 (Thedinga). Numenius was a 2nd-century Syrian Neoplatonist, a
forerunner of Plotinus.

[4] Hermippus of Berita, a Greek grammarian of the 2nd century. Cf. Eusebius, *Praeparatio evangelica* X. 1. 4; Clement, *Stromata* I. 15. 66.

[5] Webster's etymology derives the name from the Greek *aithein* and *ops*
—"to burn" and "face." Pico's reference is uncertain.

[6] Philolaus, a Pythagorean philosopher of the late 5th century B.C.

other, kept this law religiously. Lysis laments its violation by Hipparchus.[7] Finally, Porphyry is our authority that the disciples of Ammonius—Origen, Plotinus, and Herennius—swore by it.[8]

Plato himself concealed his doctrines beneath coverings of allegory, veils of myth, mathematical images, and unintelligible signs of fugitive meaning. As he himself says in his *Epistles*,[9] no one can fully understand his religious beliefs from anything he has written, and he has indeed proved this to the incredulous.

Therefore, if we think the writings of Moses commonplace because on the surface they are ordinary and crude, let us likewise condemn for ignorance and crudity all the ancient philosophers whom we venerate as masters of all knowledge. We can perceive the same practice followed in the Church. Jesus Christ, the image of the substance of God, did not write the Gospel, but proclaimed it. In fact, he proclaimed it to the crowds in parables; and separately, to the few disciples who were permitted to understand the mysteries of the kingdom of heaven, openly and without figures. He did not even reveal everything to those few, since they were not fit for everything, and there were many things which they could not endure until the coming of the spirit taught them all truth. If the few disciples of the Lord, chosen from so many thousands, could not bear so many things, could the whole people of Israel—tailors, cooks, butchers, shepherds, slaves, and maidservants, to all of whom the law was given to be read—have born the weight of the whole of Mosaic, or rather divine, wisdom? On the summit of the mountain, that very mountain on which the Lord also often addressed his disciples, the face of Moses used to become wonderously bright, illuminated by the light of the divine sun;

[7] Lysis of Tarentum and his 4th-century-B.C. contemporary, both tutors of Epaminondas. Cf. Porphyry, *Vita Pythagoras* 57 (Nauck, p. 49); Jamblichus, *Vita Pythagoras* XXVIII. 146; Philostratus, *Vita Apollonii* I. 2 ff.

[8] Porphyry, *Vita Plotini* III. 24 ff. (Brehier, p. 3). Ammonius Saccas was an Alexandrian Neoplatonist, 175-242.

[9] Plato, *Epistle II*, 312d-e.

but since the people with their owl-like and unseeing eyes could not endure the light, he used to speak to them with his face veiled.

Let us turn to the Christians. Matthew wrote the Gospel first and, as the prophet says, "hiding the words of God in his heart so that he might not sin,"[10] pursued in his account only what pertained to the humanity of Christ, lest the memory of His deeds fall into oblivion. For this reason we should understand that He is represented by a man in the mystic pageant of Ezekiel.[11] When the three Gospels had already been circulated and many years had passed since the crucifixion of our Lord, John, who compared with the others revealed the secrets of divinity in greatest measure, was compelled to speak what he had for long kept silent about the eternal generation of the Son, in order to destroy the heresy of the Ebionites,[12] who asserted Christ to be man and not God; but even he announced it obscurely and in few words, starting thus: "In the beginning was the Word."[13]

Paul denies the true food to the Corinthians because they still live by the laws of the flesh, not of the spirit, and he speaks wisdom only to the elect.[14] Paul's disciple Dionysius the Areopagite writes that it was a settled and holy custom in the churches not to communicate the more secret doctrines in writing but only by voice and to those who had been properly initiated.[15]

I have pursued this question at length because there are many who, drawing their argument from the rough bark of its words, scorn and despise the book of Moses as mediocre and trivial. Nothing is less credible to them than his having in his depths anything more divine than what he puts forth on the surface.

---

[10] Psalms 118:11.
[11] Ezekiel 8:2.
[12] An ultra-Jewish party in the early Christian church.
[13] John 1:1.
[14] I Corinthians 5:11.
[15] Pseudo-Dionysius, *Caelestis hierarchia* II (Migne, *Patrologia Graeca*, III, 133 ff.).

If this view has been sufficiently refuted, it will now be easy to believe that if he treated anywhere of the nature and making of the whole world, that is, if in any part of his work he buried the treasures of all true philosophy as in a field, he must have done so most of all in the part where avowedly and most loftily he philosophizes on the emanation of all things from God, and on the grade, number, and order of the parts of the world. On this account it was decreed by the ancient Hebrews, as Jerome records, that no one not of mature age should deal with this account of the creation of the world.[16] Therefore, perhaps I have produced a work worth the pains if, after spending a long time in very precise and laborious effort, so far as my weakness permitted, I have laid open for study the meaning of the writings of Moses.

Since I saw that many Latins and Greeks had labored on this text, besides the ancient and almost innumerable modern Chaldean[17] and Hebrew interpreters, I scarcely dared even to think of writing any new comment on the subject. On the other hand, I remembered the provision of the Mosaic law that one should not harvest his field completely but should leave a portion of it untouched so that the poor and needy might get sheaves and handfuls to satisfy their hunger.[18] When this came into my mind, I began to glean the broad fields of the Prophet with keen eyes to see whether, since the learned interpreters were no less observers of the law than interpreters, they had according to the edict of the law left any part untouched, to be harvested by us weaker men. From such a part I too might pluck for myself a few ears to place as first fruits upon the altars of the church, that I might not be shut off from the privileges of the temple like a false Israelite or one of the uninitiate. It does not follow from my offering that I can do anything which they could not, but that they, because of the precept of the law, were unwilling to block the path of study to posterity. The vastness and fertility of the field, moreover, is such that no

---

16 St. Jerome, *Epistle LIII* (Migne, *Patrologia Latina*, XXII, 547).
17 I.e., Jewish writers in Aramaic.
18 Deuteronomy 24:19.

number of harvesters can be equal to it. Even if they exerted all their strength on it with mighty and almost infinite labor, nevertheless we could still repeat the saying of the gospel, "The harvest indeed is great, but the laborers are few."[19]

Whatever, therefore, has been written on this book by holy men like Ambrose and Augustine, Strabo and Bede and Remigius,[20] and among the more recent by Aegidius and Albert,[21] and among the Greeks by Philo, Origen, Basil, Theodoretus, Apollinarius, Didymus, Diodorus, Severus, Eusebius, Josephus, Gennadius, and Chrysostom,[22] we shall leave completely untouched, since it would be both rash and superfluous for a weak man to work in that part of the field where the most robust minds have long been working. We shall make no mention at present of what Ionethes or Anchelos or the venerable Simeon[23] bequeathed in the Chaldean language, or what, among the early

[19] Matthew 9:37.

[20] Walafrid Strabo, 9th-century German poet and theologian (not the Greek geographer). Remigius of Auxerre, Benedictine monk, d. 908.

[21] Egidio Colonna, or Aegidius Romanus, Scholastic philosopher and theologian, 1247?-1316. Albert the Great, or Albertus Magnus, c. 1200-1280, Scholastic philosopher, teacher of Aquinas.

[22] Philo Judaeus, c. 30 B.C.-c. A.D. 40, leading Alexandrian Jewish philosopher who interpreted the Pentateuch allegorically in the light of Greek philosophy. Origen, c. 185-c. 254, leading Alexandrian Christian theologian. St. Basil the Great, c. 330-379, Bishop of Caesarea, orthodox theologian. Theodoretus, c. 386-457, Bishop of Cyrrhus in Syria. Apollinarius the Younger, c. 310-390, Bishop of Laodicea in Syria, leader of an heretical sect which asserted that the Logos replaced the rational human soul in Christ's human nature. Didymus, 309?-394, blind Alexandrian theologian, a follower of Origen. Diodorus, Bishop of Tarsus, d. 392. Severus, Bishop of Antioch, 511-539, leader of the Monophysite heresy. Eusebius, c. 260-340, Bishop of Caesarea in Palestine, leader of orthodox party at Council of Nicea. Flavius Josephus, 37-95?, Jewish historian writing in Greek. Gennadius, Patriarch of Constantinople, 458-471. St. John Chrysostom, c. 347-407, Patriarch of Constantinople.

[23] Ionethes is probably Jonathan ben Uzziel, or Jonathan the Chaldean, 1st-century writer of the Targum (Aramaic paraphrase) to the Prophets. Anchelos, probably Onkelos, reputed 1st-century translator of the Targum to the Pentateuch into Greek. Simeon ben Yohai, reputed 2nd-century author of the most important of all Cabalistic works, the *Zohar*, a mystical commentary on the Pentateuch.

Hebrews, Eleazar, Aba, John, Neonias, Isaac, or Joseph[24] wrote, or, among the more recent, Gersonides, Sadias, Abraam, both Moseses, Salomon, or Manaem.[25]

Going beyond all these, we shall suggest seven other interpretations of our own discovery and development, in which we shall take pains first of all to overcome, if we can, three difficulties with which all who have undertaken to expound this book seem to have had a great and difficult struggle. The first is to keep Moses from seeming to have spoken inadequately or with too little learning and wisdom. Some have escaped this difficulty on the ground that he neither spoke of all things nor imparted anything great and exalted, because he was speaking to a rude people who were not capable of understanding all things. We can believe, however, that he satisfied his rude hearers if we consider that with denser words, like a shade of horn lest their weaker eyes be strained, he covered over the light of knowledge which the wise look into. He brought the light for the benefit of healthy eyes, but he brought it screened and covered lest it hurt the bleary-eyed. He neither ought nor could nor wished to help the learned less than the unlearned.

The second difficulty is to work out a self-consistent and coherent course of interpretation and to relate to it, as if mindful

[24] There are numerous early Jewish writers of the name Eleazar; it is not certain to which Pico referred. Aba is probably Abba Aricha, c. 175-247, Jewish teacher in Babylonia. For Neonias, Garin suggests Nechunjah ben ha-Qanah late-1st-century mystical expounder of the Torah. Garin also suggests Isaac the Blind, 12th-13th-century Spanish-Provençal scholar and Cabalist.

[25] Gersonides, Levi ben Gershon, 1288-1344, philosopher attempting to reconcile Averroism with the teachings of Maimonides. Saadia ben Joseph, 882-942, Babylonian Talmudist. Abraham ben Meir ibn Ezra, 1092-1167, also referred to as Abraam the Spaniard and Abraam the Jew, Hebrew philologist and Biblical commentator, especially on the Pentateuch. Moses ben Maimon, also known as Moses the Egyptian, or Maimonides, 1135-1204, the best known of medieval Jewish philosophers, and Moses ben Nahman, also known as Moses of Gerona or Nahmanides, Spanish Talmudist, 1195-1270. Rabbi Solomon ben Isaac, or Rashi, of Troyes, 1040-1105, expounder of the Bible and Talmud. Menahem ben Benjamin of Recanati, Italy, 13th-century rabbi and Cabalist.

of a plan, a whole series in a single line from that sense in which it first began. If we introduce him as speaking perhaps of ideas, we do not wish him discussing the elements or man in the next clause. An arbitrary and violent sort of exposition, this, which it nevertheless seems, I do not say difficult, but impossible for many to avoid when commenting on this book, and which is certainly a troublesome one for all. How great the perplexity, the ambiguity, and the variety of the whole passage is! See how great a task we have conceived, which it may not be easy to carry out (May we be able to achieve it!), to interpret the entire creation of the world continuously and without confusion in not merely one but seven senses, without reference to earlier works, but producing a work completely new from the beginning!

The third difficulty is to avoid making the Prophet, or the Holy Spirit through the Prophet, assert anything strange or wonderful or alien to the nature of things as they are observed, or to the truths ascertained by the better philosophers which even men of our own faith have accepted. Why then we bring forward seven interpretations, why we undertook them, what our plan was and what necessity drove us to them, and what may be this novelty which we strive to offer, we shall make clear in the following chapter. There portraying the ideal man to write so completely on the creation of the world as to emulate nature herself, we shall try to prove that our Prophet in no way fell short of that ideal as an archetype. He attained it in all respects, so that no one else should be proposed as such an ideal, and we can all admire his greatness more easily than estimate his worth.

These labors of mine, such as they are, the first efforts of my youth thus far, are offered to you, most illustrious Lorenzo, both because they are mine and I long since dedicated and pledged myself to you, and because you provided me with the leisure of this very retreat at Fiesole in which they were born, a retreat frequently made more enjoyable by the visits, or rather the constant attendance, of your friend Angelo Poliziano, whose delightful and fertile genius now promises, I think, a fruit of philosophy as solid and mature as formerly its literary flowers were varied. It is also the custom, when something solemn or joyful happens to those whom we love or cherish, not only to congratulate them with words but also to add to their happiness with gifts, if I may speak thus, and give witness to them of the joy of our spirits. Therefore this work of my lamp-lit study comes to you opportunely, at a time when your son Giovanni[26] at an unprecedented age has been destined by the Pontiff Innocent VIII for the highest college of Christian orders, both for his native qualities, which promise all good things, and because your merits and authority ask it rightly and justly for him. It remains for us to hope that he may show himself worthy of this honor. This he will do if he takes as his model him who is both his father and the author of this honor, a model, that is, of wisdom and all virtue. Farewell.

Second Proem to the Whole Work

Antiquity imagined three worlds. Highest of all is that ultramundane one which theologians call the angelic and philosophers the intelligible, and of which, Plato says in the *Phaedrus*, no one has worthily sung.[1] Next to this comes the celestial world, and last of all, this sublunary one which we inhabit. This is the world of darkness; that the world of light; the heavens are compounded of light and darkness. This world is symbolized by water, a flowing and unstable substance; that by fire, for the splendor of its light and the elevation of its position; of a middle nature, the heavens are on that account called by the Hebrews *asciamaim*, as if composed of *es* and *maim*, that is, of the fire and water of which we spoke. Here there is an alternation of life and death; there, eternal life and unchanging activity; in the heavens, stability of life but change of activity and position. This world is composed of the corruptible substance of

---

[26] Later Pope Leo X. He was named a cardinal at the age of thirteen and formally admitted into the Sacred College at sixteen.

[1] Plato, *Phaedrus* 247c.

bodies; that one of the divine nature of the mind; the heavens of body, but incorruptible, and of mind, but enslaved to body. The third is moved by the second; the second is governed by the first; and there are among them many further differences which I do not propose to enumerate here, where we are skimming the surface of such things without fathoming their depths.

I should not pass over the fact that these three worlds were clearly diagrammed by Moses in the construction of his wonderful tabernacle. He divided the tabernacle into three parts, none of which could more expressly represent the corresponding world of which we have spoken. The first part, not protected by any roof or umbrella, was open and exposed to showers, snow, sun, heat, cold; and, to make it more obviously an image of this sublunary world of ours, there dwelt there not only clean and unclean men, the holy and the profane, but also animals of many kinds; and there was even a continuous alternation of life and death in the offerings and living sacrifices. Both the two remaining parts were protected and free from external harm on all sides, just as the celestial and supercelestial worlds are susceptible of neither injury nor harm. Both, likewise, were honored with a title of holiness, but the more secret was distinguished with the name of Holy of Holies, the other simply as the Sanctuary, just as, although the celestial and angelic worlds are both holy, because since the fall of Lucifer there neither is nor can be stain or sin above the moon, the angelic world is still held far more holy and divine than the celestial.

But why do we pursue these remote similes? For, if the outermost part of the tabernacle was common to men and animals, the second, which shone with the splendor of gold, was illuminated by a seven-branched candlestick which, as all the Latin, Greek, and Hebrew commentators declare, signifies the seven planets. In the third part, the most sacred of all, were the winged cherubim. Does not all this put the three worlds before your eyes? This one, which both men and animals inhabit; the celestial, in which the planets shine; and the supercelestial, the dwelling of the angels?

By this we are also reminded of the higher mystery of the Gospel. Since the way to the supercelestial world, to communion with the angels, was opened for us by the cross and blood of Christ, for that reason, at the moment of his death, the veil of the temple was rent asunder, the veil by which the Holy of Holies, which we have said signifies the angelic world, was separated from the other parts. This was a sign that the approach to the kingdom of God now lay open for men, the approach to God Himself, who flies above the cherubim, the approach closed off by the laws of justice from the beginning because of the sin of the first father.

This is enough on the three worlds. It should above all be observed, a fact on which our purpose almost wholly depends, that these three worlds are one world, not only because they are all related by one beginning and to the same end, or because regulated by appropriate numbers they are bound together both by a certain harmonious kinship of nature and by a regular series of ranks, but because whatever is in any of the worlds is at the same time contained in each, and there is no one of them in which is not to be found whatever is in each of the others. If we have understood him rightly, I believe that this was the opinion of Anaxagoras, as expounded by the Pythagoreans and the Platonists.[2] Truly, whatever is in the lower world is also in the higher ones, but of better stamp; likewise, whatever is in the higher ones is also seen in the lowest, but in a degenerate condition and with a nature one might call adulterated. In our world there is the elemental quality of heat, in the heavens there is a heating power, and in angelic minds there is the idea of heat. I shall speak more precisely: among us there is the fire which is an element; the sun is fire in the sky; in the ultramundane region the fire is the seraphic intellect. But see how they differ. The elemental fire burns, the celestial gives life, and the supercelestial loves. There is water in our world; there is water in the heavens, the mover and mistress of ours, namely, the moon, the vestibule of the heavens; and above

2 Simplicius, *Physica* 27. 2.

the heavens, the waters are the minds of the cherubim. But see what a disparity of condition there is in the same nature: the elemental moisture quenches the heat of life; the celestial feeds it; the supercelestial understands it.

In the first world, God, the primal unity, presides over nine orders of angels as if over as many spheres and, without moving, moves all toward himself. In the middle world, that is, the celestial, the empyrean heaven likewise presides like the commander of an army over nine heavenly spheres, each of which revolves with an unceasing motion; yet in imitation of God, it is itself unmoving. There are also in the elemental world, after the prime matter which is its foundation, nine spheres of corruptible forms. There are three of bodies without life, which are the elements and the mixtures, and then midway between them those things that are mixed but imperfect, like the storms that occur in the sky. There are three of vegetable nature, which is basically divided into the three genera of grasses, shrubs, and trees. There are three of sensitive souls, which are either imperfect as in the zoophytes, or perfect but within the limits of irrational phantasy, or what is highest among brutes, capable even of being instructed by men, a mean, as it were, between man and brute, just as the zoophyte is the mean between brute and plant.

But this is more of these things than is necessary. We shall add only this, that the mutual containment of the worlds is also indicated by the Holy Scriptures, both where it is written in the Psalms, "Who made the heavens in understanding,"[3] and where we read that the angels of God are spirits and his ministers a flame of burning fire.[4] Hence celestial or even earthly names are often given to divine things, which are presented figuratively now as stars, now as wheels and animals, now as elements; hence, also, heavenly names are often given to earthly things.[5] Bound by the chains of concord, all these worlds exchange natures as well as names with mutual liberality. From

3 Psalms 135:5 (King James, 136:5).
4 Hebrews 1:7.
5 Ezekiel 1:16 ff.

this principle (in case anyone has not yet understood it) flows the science of all allegorical interpretation. The early Fathers could not properly represent some things by the images of others unless trained, as I have said, in the hidden alliances and affinities of all nature. Otherwise there would be no reason why they should have represented this thing by this image, and another by another, rather than each by its opposite. But versed in all things and inspired by that Spirit which not only knows all these things but made them, they aptly symbolized the natures of one world by those which they knew corresponded to them in the other worlds. Therefore, those who wish to interpret their figures of speech and allegorical meanings correctly need the same knowledge (unless the same Spirit helps them also).

There is, moreover, besides the three that we have mentioned, a fourth world in which are found all those things that are in the rest. This is man himself, who is, as the Catholic doctors say, referred to in the Gospel by the name of every creature, since Christ gave the Gospel to be preached to men, not to brutes and angels, but nevertheless to be preached to every creature.[6] It is a commonplace expression in the schools that man is a lesser world, in which are seen a body compounded from the elements, and a heavenly spirit, and the vegetative soul of plants, and the sense of brutes, and reason, and the angelic mind, and the likeness of God.

Therefore, if we suppose these four worlds, it is believable that Moses, when about to speak fully of the world, should have discussed all of them; and since a writer copies nature, if he is learned about nature—as we believe this writer of ours was if anyone ever has been—it is believable that his teaching about the worlds is arranged just as God, the almighty artificer, arranged them in themselves, so that truly the scripture of Moses is the exact image of the world; just as we also read that on the mountain where he learned these things, he was commanded to make everything according to the pattern that he had seen on the mountain.[7]

6 Mark 16:15.
7 Exodus 25:40.

Therefore the first principle, which, as we have shown, is the greatest of all, is that whatever is in any of the worlds is contained in each. As the imitator of nature, Moses had to treat of each of these worlds in such a way that in the same words and in the same context he could treat equally of all. Hence there arises immediately a fourfold exposition of the whole Mosaic test, so that, in the first place, whatever is written there we interpret in relation to the angelic and invisible world, making no mention whatever of the others. In the second place, we interpret everything in relation to the celestial world; then in relation to this sublunary and corruptible one; and fourthly, in relation to the nature of man. If there is anywhere a discussion of the intelligible world, for instance, we surely can, or at least we should, interpret all the details in respect to all the others, so that just as that world contains in itself all the lower natures, so also the same passage may put us in mind of the rest of the worlds.

Although the natures are mutually contained by each other, they are nevertheless allotted their separate seats and certain peculiar rights. Likewise, although in each part of the present work the fourfold nature is treated in the same order as the text, it must be supposed that in the first part the first nature is treated more particularly, and the others in the same order in the remaining parts.

From this arises the necessity of a fifth exposition. It is added because, although these natures are distinct, there is no multiplicity which is not a unity, and they are linked together by a certain discordant concord and bound by many kinds of interwoven chains.

Since it is probable that Moses was doing this throughout his work, we are drawn in spite of ourselves to a sixth interpretation. In this we shall show that there are fifteen ways in which we can understand one thing as joined or related to another. Since there are neither more nor less, they have all been so sufficiently and clearly expressed by the Prophet that Aristotle never wrote anything more precise on the nature of things.

Finally, just as the six days of creation were followed by the

Sabbath, that is, by a rest, it is fitting that after treating the
orders of things proceeding from God and explaining their
union and diversity and their bonds and habits, we should in a
seventh, and as it were, sabbatical exposition, touch lightly on
the felicity of creatures and their return to God, which through
Mosaic and Christian law was granted to man, though we were
long separated from it through the sin of our first parent. Here
we shall disclose what in the present scripture Moses clearly
hid about these, so that this explicit prophecy of the advent of
Christ, of the increase of the Church, and of the calling of the
gentiles, may be read plainly. Thus indeed this book of Moses,
if any such, is a book marked with the seven seals and full of
all wisdom and all mysteries.

We shall not, however, imitate those who, having tried
sometimes to explain the creation of the world, have heaped
together whatever philosophers or theologians have anywhere
said about God, the angels, matter, the heavens, and the whole
of nature. Among the Hebrews, Isaac the Persian and Samuel
Ophinides[8] have particularly sinned in this. We shall take pains
only to make clear to the best of our ability what the Mosaic
scripture means, what the context of the words indicates or
signifies. If, for example, we show that by the firmament is
meant the eighth sphere, we shall not immediately begin a discussion of how it carries along the other spheres, or of how
many signs and images adorn it, or of whether it is turned by a
simple motion or rather by two or even three. If we say anywhere that the human soul is indicated by some term, we shall
avoid explaining in detail all that has been written about the
soul, but on each topic we shall only note briefly and quickly
the things which the author seems to make explicit mention
of. I say "briefly and quickly" because it is not the purpose of
this work that any who have not learned these things elsewhere
should learn them here for the first time, but that they may
recognize in the words of the Prophet what they already know

[8] Isaac the Persian, unidentifiable. Samuel Ophinides is Samuel ben
Hophni, Gaon of Sura, d. 1034, writer of Arabic commentary on the
Pentateuch.

to be true, and that, understanding how he has gathered and concealed here in a few words what they have read distributed over immense volumes by philosophers and theologians, they may listen to the lawgiver speaking with unveiled face.

If anyone, motivated perhaps by a spirit of holy simplicity, does not approve of pursuing these mysteries so deeply, but rather desires a more straightforward explanation of the sacred text more suited to himself, I shall first bid him to remember the precept of Paul, that he who eateth should not despise him that eateth not and that he that eateth not should not judge him that eateth.[9] Then I shall exhort him not in my own words but in the words of Augustine, in his own exposition of *Genesis,* as follows: "Learn these things if you can; if you cannot, leave them to your betters. Profit from a book which does not abandon your weakness and which with a motherly step walks slowly along with you; for it speaks thus to mock the proud with its loftiness, to terrify the studious with its profundity, to feed the great with its truth, to sustain the humble with its courtesy."[10]

But let us come back to ourselves and, starting with this same corruptible world in which we live, let us perform so far as possible what we have promised. In any case, "In great things it is enough to have tried,"[11] and, as Pomerius says, a great effort is the beginning of great things.[12]

The Words of Moses to be Expounded

The exact words of the Prophet that we have undertaken to expound are these:

In the beginning God created heaven and earth. And the earth was void and empty, and darkness was upon the face of the deep; and the spirit of God moved over the waters. And God said: Be light made. And light was made. And God saw the light that it was good; and he divided

9 Romans 14:3.

10 Augustine, *De Genesi ad litteram* V. 3 (6) (Migne, *P.L.,* XXXIV, 323).

11 Propertius, *Elegies* III. I. 6.

12 J. Pomerius (fl. 498), *De vita contemplativa* I, prol., 2 (Migne, *P.L.,* LIX, 415b).

the light from the darkness; and he called the light Day,
and the darkness Night; and there was evening and
morning one day.

And God said: Let there be a firmament made amidst
the waters, and let it divide the waters from the waters.
And God made a firmament and divided the waters that
were under the firmament from those that were above the
firmament, and it was so. And God called the firmament
Heaven; and the evening and morning were the second
day.

God also said: Let the waters that are under the heaven
be gathered together into one place, and let the dry land
appear. And it was so done. And God called the dry land
Earth: and the gathering together of the waters, he called
Seas. And God saw that it was good. And he said: Let the
earth bring forth the green herb, and such as may seed,
and the fruit tree yielding fruit after its kind, which may
have seed in itself upon the earth. And it was so done. And
the earth brought forth the green herb, and such as yield-
eth seed according to its kind, and the tree that beareth
fruit, having seed each one according to its kind. And God
saw that it was good. And the evening and the morning
were the third day.

And God said: Let there be lights made in the firmament of heaven, to divide the day and the night, and let
them be for signs, and for seasons, and for days, and years.
To shine in the firmament of heaven, and to give light
upon the earth. And it was so done. And God made two
great lights: a greater light to rule the day; and a lesser
light to rule the night: and the stars. And he set them in
the firmament of heaven to shine upon the earth. And to
rule the day and the night, and to divide the light and
the darkness. And God saw that it was good. And the
evening and the morning were the fourth day.

God also said: Let the waters bring forth the creeping
creatures having life, and fowl that may fly over the earth
under the firmament of heaven. And God created the
great whales, and every living and moving creature, which
the waters brought forth, according to their kinds, and
every winged fowl according to its kind. And God saw
that it was good. And he blessed them, saying: Increase
and multiply, and fill the waters of the sea: and let the
birds be multiplied upon the earth. And the evening and
the morning were the fifth day.

And God said: Let the earth bring forth the living creature in its kind, cattle and creeping things, and beasts of the earth, according to their kinds. And it was so done. And God made the beasts of the earth according to their kinds, and cattle and everything that creepeth on the earth, after its kind. And God saw that it was good. And He said: Let us make man to our image and likeness: and let him have dominion over the fishes of the sea, and the fowls of the air, and the beasts, and the whole earth, and every creeping creature that moveth upon the earth. And God created man to his own image: to the image of God He created him.[13]

We have undertaken to explain Moses thus far. I have divided the whole exposition into seven books or treatises, rather to imitate Basil and Augustine than because the integrative attention of the reader may be refreshed by frequent breaks. Moreover, since the seven expositions are arranged in seven books and each book is divided into seven chapters, the whole corresponds to the seven days of creation.

Just as with Moses the seventh day is the Sabbath and a day of rest, so we have taken care that every exposition of ours shall always in the seventh chapter be turned to Christ, who is the end of the law and is our Sabbath, our rest, and our felicity.

---

13 Genesis 1:1-27.

First Exposition

OF THE ELEMENTAL WORLD

Chapter One of the First Book

The natural philosophers who treat of the nature of corruptible things hold this in general among their first principles: that there is a crude matter devoid of form, but capable of taking on all forms, though deprived of all by its nature. Thus they make the origin of natural things privation as well as matter. Averroes added that matter is extended in three dimensions—length, breadth, and height—so that corporeal things may not be said to be made from an incorporeal substratum.[1]

Then the philosophers introduce the transmitting cause, which they call the *efficient,* by force of which the matter worked on, which is potentiality, is sometimes made something actual, just as soft and unformed wax is transformed by the molding and twisting of the hands into various shapes at the will of the molder. Moreover, since nature never acts by chance but only for the sake of some resulting good, the final cause is at once brought in, and the nearest end of the acting cause is the form, which it draws from the womb of the matter. The former works and acts upon the latter in order to bring it to the perfect state of form. Aristotle established form, therefore, as his third principle.[2] Moreover, it cannot be drawn forth from the bosom of the matter unless the matter is previously prepared and equipped with suitable qualities, on which all the labor of the workman and all the time of the action is spent, until all at once the species itself shines forth as the reward of the labor.

The Peripatetics call the workman himself a cause rather than a principle. The divine Platonists, always mindful of the

[1] Averroes, *De substantia orbis* I.
[2] Aristotle, *Metaphysics* XII. 2, 1069; *Physics* I. 6, 189a.

divine, remind us that although only natural agents seem to us to move, shape, and transform bodies, nevertheless they are by no means primary causes of the things which are made but rather instruments of a divine art which they obey and serve. In the same way, although the hands of the carpenter arrange, shape, and put together all the materials of the house—wood, stones, cement—and nothing else is seen to which the making of the finished house may be attributed, nevertheless we know that they are instruments obeying and serving the skill which, established in the mind of the architect, plans the house with all its details and builds in insensible material as soon as he conceives it. From this it comes that the Platonists themselves propose two causes, the instrumental and the ideal. The Peripatetics do not deny this but confirm it by their old saying that every work of nature is the work of intelligence.

This is what is commonly said of corruptible things, all of which Moses so included in the work of the first day that the most excellent philosophers have said nothing about them any more certain or fitting.

Chapter Two

In the beginning, therefore, he sets up two causes, the active and the material, clearly that which is in act and that which is potentiality. He calls the former heaven and the latter earth; and this interpretation of ours is confirmed by the authority of the Stoics, who called heaven the active cause and earth the material, as Varro writes,[3] not to mention the Greeks. Reason attests to this also, for matter is the most despised of all natures, as earth is of all the elements, and the agent stands to the matter in exactly the same relation as the sky to the earth, as the Peripatetics prove.

This earth, moreover, is the *void* and *empty* matter, as Jerome translates it, or *invisible* and *disordered,* as the Septuagint

[3] M. Terentius Varro (Roman historian and grammarian, 116-27 B.C.), *De lingua Latina* V. 59 (Goetz and Schoell).

puts it.[4] All these terms are suitable for a rough, unshaped matter which, destitute of all form, is deservedly said to be empty and void and which is wholly disorded and invisible. But the Hebrew terms *tou* and *bou* which we read in this place are explained differently by many Hebrews. *Tou*, indeed, they interpret as a brutish thing, senseless and dumb, and they use it to refer to the dark and misshapen appearance of matter because, when we strain for an understanding of it, it leaves us dumb; on this account Aristotle says that we know it by analogy, and Plato, by a spurious reasoning.[5]

Bou, on the other hand, by the force of the term, many explain as the rudiments and beginning of form. If we translate word for word, *bou* is the same as to say "there is in it" or "something is in it"; if we follow this interpretation, we shall understand the rudimentary form of substance, as well as its potentiality, to be in the earth. Not only did Albert[6] and many of the Peripatetics believe this, but also the ancient Hebrews, as we see clearly from the testimony of the ancient Simeon. But Moses declares how this beginning of form is to be taken by adding "and darkness was upon the face of the deep." He calls the earth the deep, that is, matter extended boundlessly in three dimensions. Above this was darkness, that is, privation, a celebrated first principle of the Peripatetics, for which no name is more fitting than darkness. Moreover, as Albert the Great constantly asserts, privation, insofar as it differs from negation, is this very beginning of form of which we spoke, and which this same philosopher has discussed fully and subtly.

Furthermore, if the earth is under the waters and, when irrigated by them, becomes pregnant with what it later brings forth, will not the waters here signify the accidental qualities and affections of matter? By their transient and fluid nature

---

[4] ἀόρατος καὶ ἀκατασκεύαστος. Cf. Aquinas, *Summa theologica*, I, q. 66, a. 2.

[5] Aristotle, *Physics* I. 7, 191a (κατ'ἀναλογίαν); Plato, *Timaeus* 52b. Cf. *Zohar*, I, 16a ff.

[6] Albertus Magnus, *Summa theologiae*, II, tr. 1, q. 4, m. 2 (*Opera*, XXXIII, 90ab); I, tr. 3, q. 15, m. 2 (*Opera*, XXX, 100a).

these even have the aspect of waters, moistened by which, as I said, matter becomes pregnant with the form which at the last moment of its time it brings to light. The Spirit of the Lord, that is, the power of the efficient cause, the instrument and tool of the Lord, is rightly said to be borne upon those waters and not upon the earth, since an agent does not touch or penetrate an object except through the medium of its qualities. When it works and acts upon these, a light arises, that is, the beauty and splendor of form, which expels and puts to flight the darkness we spoke of, that is, privation. This is done when the voice of God commands it, since natural causes do nothing which the skill of divine art has not ordained.

Thus, from the evening and the morning was made one day, since from the nature of potency and act springs a third substance which we call composite; and now the reason is clear, according to this sense, why he said "one day" and not "the first day." He rightly saw that the light was good, since the nature of form is nothing but a feeble image and a shadowy likeness of the primal good. So much, in general, for all the sorts of corruptible substance below the moon, in which we see both heaven and earth, that is, the transmuting nature and that which is transmuted, and in which we see this same earth, that is, matter, void of every sort of substance and empty likewise of all accidental form; and above this matter extending into the three-dimensional abyss we see the brooding darkness of privation, not internal to it (for privation is not the essence of matter, as Aristotle proves)[7] but covering its outer face.

Likewise above the waters, that is, the fluid tendencies present in matter as in the earth, we see borne the Spirit of the Lord, that is, the power of the active cause, not as principal cause but as the *Spirit* of the Lord, that is, the instrument of the divine art, just as our vital spirit is an organ of the mind. And at once, when the spirit worked upon those waters and persuaded the substance, by the order of God the maker, light arose, that is, the beauty and splendor of form.

---

7 Aristotle, *Physics* I. 6, 189a.

Chapter Three

Since in proper order we descend from common and general things to particulars, as Aristotle recommends,[8] Moses does likewise; after he has spoken of what is common to all elemental things, on the second day he divides all elemental substance into three parts. First, however, it must be understood that he designates all material forms here by the name of "waters," which could not be more fitting. For in this sphere of generated and corruptible things, for which matter is like the bed of the ocean, there is an unceasing flux of forms coming and going like the perpetual ebb and flow of the waves.

Certainly, as Solomon says, generation passes away and generation comes, but the earth stands forever.[9] Indeed, the Platonists, ever the imitators of Hebrew learning, call these forms generations rather than forms, because they can more truly be said to become than to be.

For this reason also, just as above he called the qualities and accidental forms of matter by the name of "waters," he will call material substances themselves by the same name in order to remind us not that the qualities themselves are substantial forms for the elements, as Alexander[10] believed, but that, as the Platonists demonstrate with great effort, every sensible appearance of matter ought to be regarded as an accident rather than as a true substance. Those things rightly claim the latter title for themselves which exist *per se,* supported by themselves, and which are with true reason what they are, unmixed, and least corrupted by other things. Heraclitus called the sea the substance of sensible things, and the poets concealed philosophy under veils of myth, when after the unitary rule of Saturn (that is, the union of the intelligible world enfolding all within it-

8 Aristotle, *Posterior Analytics* II. 13, 96b.

9 Ecclesiastes 1:4.

10 Alexander of Aphrodisias, 2nd-century commentator on Aristotle and head of the Lyceum in Athens.

self) they divided the sensible world into three parts, ascribing the celestial region to Jove, the subterranean to Pluto, and this middle one between moon and earth, which we are now discussing, to Neptune, lord of the sea, whom the Platonists interpret as the power which presides over generation.[11]

But let us go back to Moses' division of the waters from the waters by means of the firmament. The division of the sublunary bodies is threefold. Some are above the middle region of the air, namely, the highest part of this element and the purest fire, which are jointly designated by the name of ether; there the elements are pure, unmixed, and governed by law. Below the middle of the air are other bodies such as exist among us, where there are no pure elements (not even a pure sensible element), but all things are mixtures composed of the dregs and grosser parts of the body of the world.

Intervening is the region of the air, which is here called the firmament, where Moses introduces the birds, flying under the firmament of heaven. This is the region in which appear the celestial phenomena: rain, snow, lightning, thunder, comets, and the like. See how well this firmament not only by its location but also by its peculiar nature divides and distinguishes the higher elements from the lower, like the waters from the waters. Above it the elements are pure; below it, in a perfect mixture, they abandon their elemental simplicity; in it they are mixed, but imperfectly so, and in nature really intermediate between mixtures and elements.

Chapter Four

Let us see what else Moses philosophizes about. "Let the waters that are under the heaven be gathered together into one place," he says, "and let the dry land appear." Dry land is matter, as we have already established, and matter neither appears nor is seen except clothed in the likeness of forms; but it does not appear

11 Heraclitus, fr. 31. Proclus, *Theologia Platonica* VI. 22. Pletho, περὶ νόμων I. 5.

clothed in the likeness of an element since, as we have said, and as the philosophers have proved, a simple element can neither be seen nor be touched nor fall wholly under any sense. Therefore, if the earth, which was previously invisible, is about to come into sight, it is necessary for the waters which are under the heavens, that is, under the middle region of the air, to be gathered together into one place, that is, for them to flow together, compelled by certain laws as if by lictors, and to unite in a single form like the dregs of a mixture. What happens to the lower waters, as we have shown, does not happen to the higher ones, where there is either no mixture at all or only an imperfect one. But if the vegetative soul immediately follows upon the form of the mixture, what else did we expect from our philosopher than that after the gathering of the waters he should immediately bring forth the land, teeming with grasses, shrubs, and trees?

Chapter Five

It would seem that proceeding in order one ought to pass on to the animals, whose type of soul is the next after the vegetative. Nevertheless, since from the animals one goes to man, in whom ends the whole treatment of the corruptible world, Moses therefore inserted some facts about the things which are produced in the firmament and by which it is adorned, just as the earth is adorned by the things produced in it, such as metals, plants, and animals. These are the phenomena produced in the sky, that is, in the middle region of the air. Earlier Moses called this both heaven and firmament; here, however, the firmament *of* heaven, so that we may know that it is not truly heaven but what is under heaven. Therefore, also, Ennius in his *Achilles* calls this part *subiices*,[12] because it is situated next below heaven. That these phenomena, moreover, are called secondary stars, constellations, or planets by the philosophers is too well-known to be proved at more length, or to seem too far-fetched

12 Ennius, *Achilles;* cf. Nonius Marcellus, ed. Lindsay, I, 248.

to anyone if we expound in regard to them what is here said of the stars. Moreover, since all the diversity of these things is due to two primary causes, heat and cold, it will be suitable for us to ascribe those caused by heat to the sun and by cold to the moon. These phenomena assume for themselves the names of the sun, the moon, and the other stars not only because they are the same in the lower heaven as those in the more divine one, or because they appear just as bright and sparkling to men, but also because some of them follow certain constellations in the heaven as their princes and leaders. Thus they are also signs of what the constellations arousing them portend for people below. Supporting this is the fact that they follow the motion of the constellations by whose force and influence they are formed from rarefied earthly matter, that is, from vaporous exhalation.

Chapter Six

What follows about the production of animals and men is now obvious. After the plants come those hybrid things which have sense and motion, although the Pythagoreans ascribe a dull sense to plants also.[13] We shall discuss this in the reconciliation[14] which we intend to bring forth, the work of a longer examination. The animals which without any controversy participate in motion and sense are divided both here by Moses and in the *Timaeus*[15] into the flying ones and those living in the water. Highest and foremost of all is man, having reached whom the nature of the corruptible world halts and sounds a retreat.

Chapter Seven

Just as man is the absolute perfection of all lower things, so Christ is the absolute perfection of all men. If, as the philos-

[13] Aristotle, *De plantis* A. 1, 815a.
[14] Of Plato and Aristotle.
[15] Plato, *Timaeus* 39c; 40d.

ophers say, all perfection in each class is derived by the other members from the most perfect one as from a fountain, no one may doubt that the perfection of all good in men is derived from Christ as a man. To Him alone the Spirit was given without measure, so that we might all receive it from his fullness. See how without any doubt this prerogative is due to him as God and man, which also, so far as he was man, was peculiar to him and became him as a legitimate privilege.

Second Exposition

OF THE CELESTIAL WORLD

Proem to the Second Book

Let us rise from the elements to the heavens, from corruptible
bodies to the uncorrupted, so that it may be plain to all that in
the same words in which he showed us so much about the
nature of the elements the Prophet also included profound
doctrines on the heavens. When we consider this, a theory other
than that which we spoke of in the proems will become manifest to us. Why, for example, when about to speak of the active
cause and of matter, does Moses not call the former active and
the latter matter in explicit terms, instead of "sky" and "earth"?
And the dispositions of matter not qualities, as the philosophers
call them, but "waters"? And form "light" rather than "form,"
and comets and bolts of lightning and other things of that sort
not by their proper names but "stars" and "planets" and so
on with the rest?

In the introduction, of course, we offered as explanations not
only the custom of the ancients of writing occultly and figuratively of great things physical and divine, but also the ignorance
of his hearers, to whom, since they could not stand the splendor
of his teaching, Moses had to speak with a veiled face, lest those
whom he was undertaking to enlighten be blinded by too much
light. Now we have occasion for a third explanation. If he had
called matter and forms and qualities and active cause by their
right names, they could have been of service in the discussion
of the corruptible world, to be sure, but not in that of the others.
Therefore, it is a well-contrived and admirable device of
Moses, and truly carried out with divine rather than human
diligence, to use terms and to arrange his discourse so that the
same words, the same context, and the same order in the whole

passage are completely suitable for symbolizing the secrets of all the worlds and of the whole of nature. It is in this respect that the book of Moses excels all other progeny of the human mind in doctrine, eloquence, and genius, and this is the new and hitherto untouched aspect which we have tried to present, in order by the facts themselves to prove to men of our time that Moses did this.

This is the model, this is the pattern for perfection in a writer. Not only, as we showed above, does this kind of writing copy and emulate nature, but also, among the Scriptures, that is greatest and holds the apex of all perfection which in the fewest words both fittingly and deeply encompasses all things as well as single things. Similarly among angelic minds, according to the authority of Dionysius and St. Thomas, the glory of our theology, that is highest which by its intelligence understands with the fewest concepts and forms what lower minds understand with many and varied ones.[1] But why do we longer delay the Prophet's coming forward with unveiled face to speak to us of the heavenly mysteries? Nevertheless, before we hear him speak himself, in order to be more capable of understanding his words it will be useful for us to introduce a few remarks on the tenth heaven.

Chapter One

Above the nine spheres of the heavens, that is, the seven planets and the eighth sphere, which is called that of the fixed stars, and the ninth sphere, which is apprehended by reason, not by sense, and which is first among the bodies that move, there is believed to be a tenth heaven, fixed, quiet, and at rest, which does not participate in motion. This has been believed not only by Christians, especially recent thinkers like Strabo and Bede,[2]

1 Pseudo-Dionysius, *Caelestis hierarchia* VII; Aquinas, *Summa theologica*, I, q. 89, a. 1.

2 W. Strabo, *Glossa ordinaria in Genesim*, I, 1 (Migne, *P.L.*, CXIII, 68c); Bede, *In Pentateuch* (Migne, *P.L.*, XCI, 192).

but also by many Hebrews, and by certain philosophers and mathematicians. Let it be enough to bring forward two of these, Abraam the Spaniard, a great astrologer, and Isaac the philosopher,[3] both of whom confirm this.

This Isaac takes the tenth sphere to be what Ezekiel designated as the sapphire in the likeness of a throne, since the color of the sapphire signifies the splendor of its light, the likeness to a throne its immobility.[4] He likewise takes the ten spheres to be what Zachariah represented by the seven-branched golden candlestick, the lamp above it, and the two olive trees above the lamp.[5] Since the seven lights indicate the seven planets, and the lamp the eighth circle shining with so many sources of light, he wishes the ninth and tenth spheres to be indicated by the two olive trees, because the oil from the olives flows to the lamp and to the branches of the candlestick to feed the lights. By similarity of pattern, since the light of the visible heaven emanates and is maintained from the highest heavens (for what gives light also maintains it), the latter are properly compared to the olives, the former to the candlestick and the lamp.

But if two primary sources cannot be assigned to the same stream, one of the two highest spheres must be the first principle of all light. If light is to be traced back to one sphere as to its source, that is, to the tenth, which is then the unity of lights, then the ninth may be first to receive the light with the whole essence of its substance. In the third stage, it may come with full participation to the sun, and then from the sun in the fourth and last stage it may be divided among all the stars. Therefore above the nine heavens let us suppose a tenth, which the theologians call the empyrean.

Some doubt whether its nature be corporeal or not rather incorporeal, since it is perhaps fitting for the unity of something, corresponding by an analogy of nature to the elemental number, not to be of the same sort as the thing. But whatever

[3] Abraam, see above, n. 25, p. 73. Isaac ben Solomon Israeli, 9th-century Jewish physician and philosopher in Egypt and Tunisia.
[4] Ezekiel 1:26.
[5] Zachariah 4:2-3.

may be concluded on this question, let it remain unshaken that the treasuries of light are there and that from them as from a primal fountain whatever light is found and beheld in bodies is drawn off. And it does not matter if anyone wishes to believe more obstinately than truly that it is not of a truly corporeal nature, since in the theology of the Phoenicians, as the Caesar Julian writes in his oration on the sun,[6] it is held that corporeal light emanates from an incorporeal nature. Therefore this sphere governs the nine coming beneath it in descending order, as a general his army or a form its matter; and exhibiting the image of unity, it completes the group of ten.

Chapter Two

Let us come back to Moses, who, preparing to speak of all things, deemed this sphere, as if the first and foremost, peculiarly worthy of the name of "heaven." In the same way we may call the nine choirs of angels gods because they participate in divinity, from which comes the expression "God of gods," but when we say "God" in an absolute sense we do not understand one of them but the indivisible Trinity presiding over them, just as the empyrean heaven presides over the nine orbits subject to it. He called the eight lowest spheres earth, moreover, and not without cause, since the extremes of this group claim for themselves the name of earth. These are the moon and the starry heaven, both of which we are compelled to call earth, both by the authority of the ancients and by reason. It was very common in the Academy to give the eighth sphere the name of earth. Aristotle likewise said the moon was like the earth, doubtless imitating the Pythagoreans, who call it both the heavenly earth and the earthly heaven.[7] See how reason leads us to both conclusions. If we seek the elements in the sky, we consider as earth the moon, the lowest and most ignoble of all the stars, just as earth is lowest of all the elements, and very

6 The Emperor Julian (331-363), *Opera*, ed. Hertlein, I, 171-175.
7 Aristotle, fr. 204 (Rose).

similar to the earth in the opacity of its substance and in its
blemishes. Then for water we take Mercury, a shifting star that
changes its form, and therefore called by Lucan the lord of the
tide; for air, Venus, giving life by its tempered warmth; and for
fire, the Sun, for very obvious reasons. Then, in inverse order,
Mars for fire; Jupiter, related in nature to Venus, for air; for
water, Saturn, aged by pernicious cold; it remains for us to call
the eighth and unwandering sphere earth, as the very order of
the computation demands. Therefore all this which is included
on either hand by the two earths, above which there is nothing
visible to us, Moses correctly calls earth. Then he adds "and
the earth was void and empty," obviously through the lack of
light, not yet extended to it from the first heaven, and of the
rest of the virtues of which light is the vehicle.

We do not say this on our own authority, for the author himself declares what is lacking, as he adds "and darkness was upon
the face of the deep," rightly calling "the deep" the great and
extraordinary difference of altitude of so many orbs. Lest we
should believe there to be nothing between the eighth sphere
and the seat of the empyrean, as many have believed, following
merely the evidence of the senses, he reminds us of the intervening orb, which he himself symbolized by waters and which
is fitly called by later writers the crystalline heaven. Above this
was borne or, as Hebrew wisdom has it and as Ephraim the
Syrian[8] translates it, "brooded," the Spirit of the Lord; that is,
the closely adhering spiritual Olympus, the seat of the Spirits
of the Lord, warmed it with its life-giving light,[9] and it is well
that that which holds fast to the source of light with its whole
body and its whole bulk should drink up the light, even though
invisible to us, since the light is not limited by a more solid
body. Therefore, in the beginning, the brooding empyrean was
lavishing upon that sphere its own light, which, after the shadows had been cast out at God's command, was soon drawn off
into the other spheres which we have said were designated as

[8] 306-373, Biblical commentator and hymn writer.
[9] Augustine, *De Genesi ad litteram* I. 18 (36) (Migne, *P.L.*, XXXIV, 260).
Cf. Basil, *Homilia II in Hexaëmeron*.

"the earth" and "the deep," and the evening and the morning were made one day, since through the reception of light and supernal influence the lower heavens were allied to the first. Thus both the pre-eminence of the first heaven over the rest and the transference of light from it to them were briefly indicated on the first day, and by the names of water and earth were indicated many things concerning the peculiarities of the ninth sphere and of the others.

Chapter Three

Speaking now more particularly of the moving orbs, Moses teaches that the sphere of the fixed stars, which we call the firmament, is midway between two bodies of water. The reason for this statement is clear from what we have said, for as we have demonstrated, both the ninth sphere and the planet Saturn claim for themselves the name of waters.

The firmament was placed by God in the midst of the waters, and the waters which are under the heaven were gathered together into one place, and it was done so that dry land might appear, that is, the earth, and all this was attended to for the welfare of living things. Let us see what these words of Moses mean. The waters which are under the heaven are the seven planets, of which the first is Saturn, which are under the firmament which he has called heaven. These waters were gathered into one place because all the virtue of the planets is collected in the sun alone; the philosophers and mathematicians confirm this unanimously. If this gathering of the waters is called the sea, not irrationally will it be that ocean which is called, by those who honored the planets with the names of gods, the father of gods and men.

Moreover, what shall we call earth but the moon, so named by Aristotle and the Pythagoreans? It is neither useful nor visible to us when it is covered by the waves of the above-mentioned sea, but is suitable both for animal uses and for ours when, withdrawing from that sea, it comes more and more into view.

Then become fertile and fruitful those things of a vegetable nature, whose functions are growth, nutrition, and generation; for the peculiar power of the moon when it appears makes it the generator of grasses, shrubs, and trees, as the Chaldeans held and as Moses also here clearly demonstrates. See how he has shown us the nature of the moon and the sun figuratively and in a few words. But why is he silent about the rest, when we promised in our proems that he would treat sufficiently and learnedly of all? Why, I say, when he has made mention of the tenth, ninth, and eighth spheres, and also of Saturn, the sun, and the moon, is there not even a word of the four that are left, Venus and Mercury, Jupiter and Mars?

Perhaps you will say that he did it because a rude people is acquainted only with the sun and moon. But I have deprived myself of this refuge, and I cannot without blushing betake myself to it, since I swore that Moses omitted nothing which might make for a perfect understanding of all the worlds. Let someone else say that what has been asserted of the sun and moon has been asserted of the rest, since these two planets hold dominion over the heavens and exercise a universal influence, while the virtue of the other planets is particular. But not even this interpretation satisfies us, and by the same reasoning Moses ought to have omitted Saturn, which we have shown that he mentions.

I believe that yet more deeply hidden here lies a mystery of the ancient wisdom of the Hebrews, among whose dogmas on the heavens this is important: that Jupiter and Mars are included by the sun, and Venus and Mercury by the moon. If we weigh the natures of these planets, the reason for this belief is not obscure, although the Hebrews themselves offer no reason for the doctrine.

Jupiter is hot, Mars is hot, and the sun is hot, but the heat of Mars is angry and violent, that of Jupiter beneficent, and in the sun we see both the angry violence of Mars and the beneficent quality of Jupiter, that is, a certain tempered and intermediate nature blended of these. Jupiter is propitious, Mars of ill omen, the sun partly good and partly bad, good in its radiation, bad in conjunction. Aries is the house of Mars, Cancer the dignity of Jupiter: the sun, reaching its greatest height in Cancer and its greatest power in Aries, makes clear its kinship with both planets.

Let us come to the moon, which clearly shares in the waters of Mercury, and shows how great an affinity it has with Venus by the fact that in Taurus, the house of Venus, it is so exalted that it is judged to be nowhere more propitious or beneficent. Thus Moses has spoken sufficiently so far of the empyrean heaven, the ninth sphere, the firmament, the planet Saturn, and the sun and the moon which represent the rest, suggesting their inclusion to us by his very silence.

Chapter Four

After Moses had spoken of the nature of the planets, it remained for him to discuss their working and their functions, stating for what use they had been assigned. Know, moreover, that thus far the heavens have been treated as luminous bodies and that nothing has been said by the Prophet of their intelligence or of their motive force, an order which the *Timaeus* also follows, first constructing the body and then adding the soul to the completed body. In general there are two obvious activities of the heavenly bodies: motion and illumination. A double motion is established: one of the whole world, by which the heavens and the ether revolve through the whole space of the universe in a complete circuit in twenty-four hours; the other proper to the stars, manifold and various, among which the principal is the motion of the sun, which circles through all the signs of the Zodiac in the space of twelve months. The former makes the day and is therefore called diurnal; the latter makes the year; the other motions of the stars are completed in various intervals of time. Correctly and briefly therefore Moses reminded us of all this when he said that the stars were

placed in the firmament for days, years, and seasons; he added
"for signs," which I pass over because it is sufficiently explained
by other interpreters.

Moreover he expressly indicated the remaining work of the
stars, which is illumination, when he said that they were created to shine in heaven and to give light upon the earth. Although there are differing opinions among the ancients as to
what influence the heavenly bodies have upon those below, the
words of Moses fall aptly whatever opinion one holds. If they
exercise their influence only by their light, as Aristotle seems
to have meant, if we interpret his words strictly and not according to our own whims, nothing more consistent with the
statements of Moses can be conceived. If they exert influence
also by their heat, but not in any other way, as Averroes the
Arab and Abraam the Jew have it, it was enough to have
spoken of their light, from which these authors show that heat
is produced. If many and manifold other virtues are also shed
upon us from the heavens, as it seemed to Avicenna and the
Babylonians, mention of the light alone was not made by
chance, since, as Avicenna himself writes,[10] it is light alone
which conveys all the rest of the virtues to us from heaven.
Therefore the bodies of the moon, sun, and stars have been assigned to these services.

Chapter Five

It was left for Moses to mention both the constellations which
are visible in the zodiac and those in the crystalline heaven
which, although not seen by us, are nevertheless more powerful. Concerning the latter, nothing thus far has been said; therefore the animals which the waters and the earth produce
represent them, especially the waters above the heavens, and
the earth, which is the firmament itself, as was proved above.
The constellations which are seen only in those two spheres, in

[10] Avicenna, *De caelo et mundo* 14. Cf. Aquinas, *II Sententiarum*, d. 13,
q. 1, a. 3.

the form of animals such as we find amongst us, were observed by the Egyptians and the Indians, who, aided by the flatness of their land and the calmness of their skies, could discover them more easily and correctly than men of our country. Otherwise, the production of mortal animals does not concern these two elements, earth and water, more than the others, fire and air. Since Moses gave the name of water to the crystalline sphere, he fittingly called the animals there fish, and those in the firmament, which he called earth, cattle and beasts.

Chapter Six

So much for the corporeal nature of the heavens. Now, about to declare them possessed of a rational soul, Moses uses man as an allegory, not the frail and earthly creature which we see, but the one by which, as Plotinus says,[11] the visible man is governed. This is the rational soul itself, which in the *Timaeus* is formed of the same elements and in the same mixing bowl as the soul of the heavens,[12] and not incongruously what is said of the soul of man is carried over to the soul of the heavens. The Holy Scriptures, in which all angelic and rational natures are often represented by man, agree with our interpretation. This usage is very common in the prophets for the good angels, and also for the evil demon, who does not differ from them at all in nature. It is written in the Gospel: "A hostile man hath done this."[13] God added to the heavenly mechanism a living and rational substance, partaking of intellect; and therefore He wished it, because of its resemblance and likeness, to rule over those creatures which we mentioned above, the starry constellations and the planets, which revolve at its nod and obey its word without delay or stubbornness. In irrational bodies made

11 Plotinus, *Enneads* I. 1. 10.

12 Plato, *Timaeus* 41d.

13 Matthew 13:28. The Douay version gives "enemy" rather than "hostile man," but the Latin is *inimicus homo,* which gives more point to Pico's comment.

of elements this does not happen in an equal degree. You will scarcely find anything over which the Peripatetics sweat more than to prove that no heavenly body resists its mover as our bodies resist us. They are not wearied, distressed, or fatigued by perpetual motion as we would be. This is the power, which Moses touches on, of the heavenly man over the animals.

Likewise it is not without mystery why God created that man male and female. It is the prerogative of the heavenly souls to perform simultaneously both the function of contemplation and that of governing their bodies, and the latter cannot hinder or be an obstacle to the former, nor the former to the latter. It was commonly the practice of the ancients, as we observe in the Orphic hymns, to designate by the terms *male* and *female* these two powers in the same substance, one of which is engaged in contemplation while the other rules the body.[14]

These are the things related by the Prophet of the celestial world, that is, of its divine body, of the number of its spheres, of its nature, its properties, its function, and finally of its motive power, its rational substance, and its intelligence.

Chapter Seven

We should honor and exalt this noble creation. If, however, we have not forgotten the Platonic notion we mentioned—not to speak of the theologians—that the Divine Artificer compounded our souls in the same mixing bowl and of the same elements as the celestial souls, let us take care not to wish ourselves the slaves of those whom nature wished to be our brothers. Let us not measure our stature by our feeble bodies. As it is written in the *Alcibiades,* man is not this weak and earthbound thing we see, but a soul, an intelligence, which transcends all the boundaries of heaven and all the passage of time.[15]

Therefore we ought to beware lest, like many assigning and attributing to heaven more than is necessary, we resist the will

14 Damascius, *De principiis* 123 (Ruelle, I, 317).
15 Plato, *Alcibiades I,* 124ab.

of the Artificer and the order of the universe and, while seeking to please, actually displease the very heaven which has the plans of God and the order of the world much at heart. The Chaldeans remind us of this, saying, "Do not exaggerate fate."[16] Jeremiah asserts this. "Do not be afraid," he says, "of the signs of heaven, which the heathens fear."[17] Our prophet teaches this elsewhere, reminding us that man should beware lest, honoring the sun, moon, and stars, he worship what God created for the service of all peoples.[18] Although some may not accept this in the sense that the stars should serve us like base and mortal bodies, nevertheless we shall understand it to mean that the lords and authors of our nature cannot be substances of which parts are even baser than the more ignoble parts of us. There neither can nor ought to be anything in the product more perfect than in the maker.

Therefore let us fear, love, and reverence Him in whom, as Paul says, all things were created, visible and invisible.[19] He is the beginning in whom God created heaven and earth, the Christ. He himself, when asked who he was, replied, fully aware of himself, "I am the beginning who speak to you."[20] Let us not shape images of the stars in metals but an image of him, the Word of God, in our souls. Let us not seek from the heavens goods of body or fortune, which they will not give, but from the Lord of heaven, the Lord of all good things, to Whom is given all power in heaven and earth, let us seek both present goods, so far as they are good, and the true felicity of eternal life.

[16] *Oracula Chaldaica,* ed. Kroll, p. 50.
[17] Jeremiah 10:2.
[18] Deuteronomy 17:3.
[19] Colossians 1:16.
[20] John 8:25.

Third Exposition

OF THE ANGELIC AND
INVISIBLE WORLD

Proem to the Third Book

Thus far we have discussed the celestial world, unveiling the mysteries of Moses to the best of our ability. Who will now give me the wings of a dove, wings covered with silver and yellow with the paleness of gold?[1] I shall fly above the heavenly region to that of true repose, peace, and tranquility, especially that peace which this visible and corporeal world cannot give. Unveil my eyes, you ultramundane spirits, and I shall contemplate the wonders of your city, where God has laid up for those who fear him what the eye has not seen, nor the ear heard, nor the heart thought.

Since much about the angelic and invisible nature has been handed down by the ancient Hebrews and much also by Dionysius, it was my plan to expound the words of Moses according to the teaching of both schools. But since what is said by the Hebrews is unfamiliar to the Latins and could not easily be understood by our people unless, hatched from a twin egg, as they say, I explained nearly all of the dogmas of the ancient learning of the Hebrew people, I thought I ought to put it off until I have made these dogmas known to my countrymen by writing of them more fully elsewhere, examining how far they agree with the traditions of Egypt, the philosophy of Plato, and Catholic truth. If they agree with us anywhere, we shall order the Hebrews to stand by the ancient traditions of their fathers; if anywhere they disagree, then drawn up in Catholic legions we shall make an attack upon them. In short, whatever

[1] Psalms 54:7 (King James, 55:6).

106

we detect foreign to the truth of the Gospels we shall refute to the extent of our power, while whatever we find holy and true we shall bear off from the synagogue, as from a wrongful possessor, to ourselves, the legitimate Israelites.

Meanwhile, treading in the footsteps of Dionysius, or rather Paul and Hierotheus,[2] whom he followed, we shall try to the extent of our weakness to bring light upon those shadows of the law which the Spirit of God, the author of law, set up for his hiding place.[3]

Chapter One

Any number, after unity, is perfected and completed by unity. Unity alone, completely simple, perfected by itself, does not go beyond itself but in its individual and solitary simplicity is composed of itself, since it is self-sufficient, in want of nothing, and full of its own riches. Since number by its nature is manifold, it is simple—so far as it is capable of simplicity—only by virtue of unity; and although every number falls into ever greater multiplicity the further it is removed from unity, and the more diversity, the more parts, and the more compoundness there is in it; nevertheless, none is so close to unity as not to be a multiple, having only an accidental unity and being one not by nature but by composition.

Let us apply these notions to divine things, after the Pythagorean custom. God alone, who is derived from nothing and from whom all things are derived, is a wholly simple and individual essence. Whatever he has, he has from himself. For the same reason that he exists, he knows, wills, and is good and just. We cannot understand any reason why he exists except that he is being itself. Other things are not being itself, but exist by means of it.

Therefore an angel is not unity itself, or else he would be God, or there would be many gods, which cannot even be con-

2 Fictitious mystic referred to as historical by the Pseudo-Dionysius.
3 Psalms 17:12 (King James, 18:11).

ceived. For what will be one if not unity? It is left for an angel
to be a number. But if it is, it is a number in one aspect and one
multiplicity in another. Every number, however, is imperfect
insofar as it is a multiplicity, but perfect so far as it is one.
Therefore, whatever is imperfect in an angel let us ascribe to
the angel's multiplicity, which it has from being a number, that
is, a creature; and whatever is perfect to its participation in
unity, which it has from being associated with God.

In an angel we find a double imperfection: the one, that it is
not being itself but only an essence to which being comes by
participation, so that it *may* be; the other, that it is not intelligence itself but only *happens* to understand, since by its
nature it is an intellect capable of understanding. The second
imperfection, however, depends on the first, since what does not
exist of itself, certainly does not understand by itself, since there
can be nothing where being itself is not. Therefore both of
these imperfections befall an angel insofar as it is a multiplicity.
It remains for its perfection and completion to be produced by
unity coming from above. God is the unity from which angels
draw their being, their life, and all their perfection.

Just as the imperfection is double, as if a double multiplicity,
so let us understand a double approach toward unity so that
both may be perfected. The first is that by which there exists
the crude and unformed essence devoid of life and being, that
is, the void and empty earth which God created. Do not believe,
as many have believed, that only the formation of essence is
the work of the Artificer, and not its creation also. At the same
time as the earth He created the heavens, that is, the actuality
of that essence and the unity which is shared in multiplicity,
that is, being itself, so that the creation of heaven and earth is
almost the same as that of a mutual embrace or of two natures
adapted through a similar bond to the same end. It is not out
of keeping with the ancients for us to call being itself heaven,
a participation in divinity, when Xenophanes called the arch-
etypal world a sphere[4] and both the Saracens and our own
people call God a circle.

4 Aristotle, *De Melisso, Xenophane, et Gorgia* 3, 977b.

Chapter Two

An angel, from what we have said, has perfectly realized his own nature and intellectual qualities. Nevertheless, he does not have a way to fulfill his functions of understanding and contemplation unless he is first surrounded by God with intelligible forms. For this reason the darkness has hitherto been upon the face of the deep. The deep is his intellectual capacity, penetrating and searching everything profound. Above this is the darkness, until it is illuminated by the rays of spiritual concepts by which he sees and contemplates everything. It is written, however, "upon the face of the deep," not "upon the deep," because the same place is one of darkness and of light. The light of intelligible forms covers the face, the exterior of the angelic intelligence, because their qualities are accidental to it and do not pertain to its essence. After the darkness has been driven way, Moses adds whatever may occur before the light arises by saying, "And the Spirit of God moved over the waters."

What will the Spirit of the Lord be other than the spirit of love? We cannot with propriety say that the spirit of knowledge is the Spirit of the Lord, because knowledge sometimes leads away from God. Love, however, always leads us to God. If it is not borne upon the deep, light will not be made, since just as the eye is not filled with light unless turned toward the sun, so an angel is not filled with the spiritual light unless turned toward God. This turning movement is not, and can not be, anything in the angelic nature but the motion of love.

Therefore it was the Spirit of the Lord, the spirit of love, that was borne upon the deep, that is, upon the angelic intellect (for love follows understanding). Driven and excited by it, the mind of the angel turns toward God. God said "Be light made," and light was made in the angel, the light of intelligible forms; and the evening and the morning were one day since, as Averroes shows, from the intellect and the intelligible is made a greater unity than from matter and form, because, as the same author affirms and as Moses the Egyptian also writes, truth is grasped far better by angels than by men.[5] To pass over those writers, let this reason be enough for us—that intelligible species are united to angelic minds by eternal links and an indivisible bond, not a vague and customary one as happens with the human intellect.

Chapter Three

We have seen the nature of the angels created by God, turned to God by the spirit of love, and then enlightened by him and perfected by the light of intelligible forms. Let us now see into what ranks the angelic armies are divided.

We read that the firmament was placed in the midst of the waters, by which are indicated to us the three hierarchies of angels (for thus we shall always call them, by the customary word). The first and last of these are designated by the waters, the former by those above the heavens, the latter by those which are under the heavens; the middle one dividing them is called the firmament. All this, if we consider the nature and duties of the three hierarchies, could not be more in accord with the teaching of Dionysius. Since, as he writes,[6] the highest hierarchy has leisure only for contemplation, it is properly symbolized by the waters that are placed above the heavens, that is, above all action in regard to worldly things, whether heavenly or earthly, and they praise God unceasingly with everlasting sound. Since the middle rank is assigned to the work of the heavens, it could not be more fittingly symbolized than by the firmament, that is, the sky. The final hierarchy, although by nature it is above everybody and above the heavens, nevertheless has charge of things under the heavens. Since it is divided into principalities, archangels, and angels, all the activity of these is concerned only with what is under the moon; that of the principalities

---

[5] Averroes, *De animae beatitudine* (ed. Giunta [1573], IX, 153ab).
[6] Pseudo-Dionysius, *Caelestis hierarchia* VII ff.

with states and kings and princes, as we learn from Daniel,[7] that of the archangels with mysteries and holy ceremonies; the angels are busy with private affairs and are assigned to men individually. Therefore this subcelestial army, which presides over transitory and perishable things and is beneath the rank engaged with heavenly things, is symbolized by the subcelestial waters.

Chapter Four

What it may be for the waters under the heavens to be gathered together into one place would perhaps be doubtful if it were not explained to us by Paul, in whom we read that the angels sent to carry on the duties of this world are all guardian spirits sent to minister to those who receive the inheritance of salvation.[8] From this we can understand that these subcelestial waters, that is, the angelic armies, have been assembled into one place to look after the good and salvation of man alone. For this they are sent to us and appear to us in different forms and places and times, now after our going to sleep and now when we are awake.

How this doctrine should be received we shall learn when we have turned our minds to how what Moses says may be true, namely, that the waters were gathered together into one place. For that statement is not true in the sense that waters may nowhere be found in distinct and separate places, since the Indian sea is divided by a great distance from the Hyrcanian,[9] the Hyrcanian from the Adriatic, the Adriatic from the Euxine, and the countless currents of rivers, fountains, and lakes from each other. But the waters are said to be gathered into one place because these particular and divided collections of sea or river waters, all flowing toward the primary sea, as Solomon says,[10]

[7] Daniel 7.
[8] Hebrews 1:14.
[9] The Caspian Sea.
[10] Ecclesiastes 1:7.

are united and come together into the one place of the ocean. Scarcely otherwise should we understand the angels which have charge of sublunary things. Different ones preside over different corporeal and non-human things, since, just like the Platonists, our philosophers also have believed that God placed various spiritual substances in authority over the various things in this corruptible world. Augustine also asserted, as Gregory later confirmed, that there is no visible thing among us over which an angelic power does not preside, and that all bodies are constantly ruled by a rational spirit of life.[11] Origen likewise, in his commentary on the book of Numbers, says that the world needs angels to preside over animals and their birth and also over the increase of bushes and plantings and other things.[12]

The Damascene[13] was also of this opinion, believing that the angel who sinned was one of those of the most contemptible kind who preside over the terrestrial order. Just as all things below man are considered in relation to him, so all the care, toil, and zeal of the angels for these things is chiefly subordinated to his benefit, so that they may attend to human affairs and, aiding our weakness, see to it that so far as we ourselves allow it, we live our lives piously and happily.

Therefore what that gathering of the waters means, Moses at once introduces: that the earth may yield fruit, grass, plants, and trees. What is this earth but that of which it is written in the Gospel that some brings forth fruit a hundredfold, some sixty, and some thirty?[14] The earth, especially, of our souls, of which Paul writes these words: "The earth that drinketh in the rain that cometh often upon it, and bringeth forth herbs meet for them by whom it is tilled, receiveth blessing from God. But that which bringeth forth thorns and briers is reprobate, and very near unto a curse, whose end is to be burnt."[15] Therefore

11 Augustine, *De diversis quaestiones* LXXXIII. I. 79 (Migne, *P.L.*, XL, 90). Cf. St. Gregory, *In Ezechiel* I. 7.
12 Origen, *In Hieremias* VIII (Migne, *Patrologia Graeca*, XIII, 364-365).
13 St. John of Damascus, d. *c.* 752.
14 Matthew 13:8.
15 Hebrews 6:7-8.

let us also take care that our earth yield fruit in its time, that it yield purgative virtues like herbs, knowledge and wisdom like the taller shrubs, and absolute and perfect virtue like the cedars of Lebanon, that its end may be a blessing and not a burning. Let us hear the Father saying: "Behold, the smell of my son is as the smell of a plentiful field, which the Lord hath blessed."[16] And let no one be astonished that the heaven and earth signify one thing for us on the first day and the firmament and the dry land something else now, as we also observed in the preceding books, when Basil and Origen and many others want the heaven and earth to be one thing for Moses on the first day and the firmament and the dry land something else on the second.[17]

Chapter Five

Even the heavenly powers favor this earth of ours, for the sun, moon, and stars were placed in the firmament to give light to our earth. See how aptly this agrees with the mysteries of Dionysius. We have spoken of the lowest hierarchy, the one assigned to the care of sublunary, that is, human affairs. Now we are concerned with the middle one, to which is entrusted the administration of heavenly matters. We should not expect to treat similarly of the third, of which there is nothing to be said beyond what has been said, namely, that it is above the heavens, that is, above all active motion and above the administration of all worldly things, given only to contemplation. In this place, however, let us not judge it extravagant nor foreign to the Holy Scriptures that Moses calls "sun" and "moon" not the stars which we see, but the angelic powers which govern the sun and moon. The Scripture also, when it says that man is made the son of God through grace, does not mean the frail and perishable man which we see, but that which rules what we see.

In the history of the kings, according to the Hebrew text,

[16] Genesis 27:27.

[17] Basil, *Hexaëmeron* III. 3 (Migne, *P.G.*, XXIX, 56-60); Origen, *In Genesim* I. 1-2 (Migne, *P.G.*, XII, 145-148).

we read of Solomon praying in these words: "Hear me, oh heaven,"[18] when nevertheless he was calling not upon heaven but upon the lord and ruler of heaven and earth. Therefore here also, when we hear of the sun and the stars, let us understand not the stars, but the angels presiding over the stars, who, since they are invisible themselves, illuminate an earth which is also invisible, namely, the substance of our souls. Moreover, it is not said either rashly or vulgarly that the stars were created to give light, but so properly, and so harmoniously with the passages which we have brought forward, that by these if by nothing else our interpretation will be strongly confirmed. For since, as Dionysius says,[19] there are three angelic activities, purification, illumination, and perfection, they are so distributed that the lowest order purifies, the highest perfects, and the middle one, which we are now discussing, illuminates. Therefore the lower waters purify our earth so that it becomes bright in appearance; the heavenly ones illuminate it when purified; the supercelestial ones perfect it with a fiery and life-giving dew, and often fertilize it for such great felicity that there germinate not healthful herbs but the Savior himself, and not one virtue is formed in us, but Christ, the fullness of all virtues.

Chapter Six

Moses goes on to say that from the elements there sprang a multitude of inhabitants, fish, birds, and beasts. At this I would truly be in greater perplexity than anywhere else in this work if there did not come to my aid both Isaiah, in whom we read of the winged Seraphim,[20] and Ezekiel, according to whom, if we believe the Hebrews, the birds and beasts symbolize spiritual substances. Moreover, the ancient Hebrews, all of whom hold that Moses here intended the angelic host, hasten to assist me. Let us say, therefore, following their footsteps, that here the

18 I Kings 8:32.
19 Pseudo-Dionysius, *Caelestis hierarchia* XI.
20 Isaiah 6:2.

Prophet refutes the error of the philosophers who believed that there are certain princely intellectual substances but denied that each of them is set over a numerous multitude of lower rank, like the commander of a legion, as the theologians say. Since we know of nine orders of angels, and since each order has chosen its own leader by lot, let us fashion that leader and prince in our minds as a great sphere, and then the following army as the inhabitants and ornament of that sphere, just as we think of the fish in the water, the birds in the air, the beasts on the land, and the stars in the eighth sphere. Then that saying of Daniel will be true: "Ten thousand stood before him, and a thousand thousands ministered unto him."[21]

Chapter Seven

Finally Moses mentions man, not because man is an angel, but because he is the end and terminus of the angelic world, just as when discussing corruptible nature he presents man not as part of that nature, but as its beginning and head. From this it comes that the discussion of man pertains to the three worlds, to that which is proper to him and to both extremes, the incorporeal and the elementary, between which he is placed so that he is the end of one and the beginning of the other. But I see a trap prepared for our interpretation, since it may be pointed out that man is set over the fish of the sea, the birds, and the beasts. If these signify the angelic natures, how can what is written be true, that over them is set man, who, the philosophers know and the Prophet testifies, is lower than the angels?[22] Let Him who also ground Satan under our feet, Jesus Christ, the first-born of all creatures, aid us and destroy the trap. He surely destroys the trap and loosens and bursts every knot, not only because in Him, in Whom all divinity dwelt corporeally, human nature is so elevated that Christ as a man, so far as He is man, teaches, enlightens, and perfects the angels, if

21 Daniel 7:10.
22 Psalms 8:6 (King James, 8:5).

we believe Dionysius,[23] being made according to Paul much better than the angels,[24] as He inherited a more excellent name than they; but also because all of us, to whom the power is given to become sons of God through the grace whose giver is Christ, can be raised to an honor above that of the angels.

[23] Pseudo-Dionysius, *Caelestis hierarchia* IV.
[24] Hebrews 1:4.

Fourth Exposition

THAT IS, OF THE HUMAN WORLD: OF THE NATURE OF MAN

Proem to the Fourth Book

After we have shown that the Prophet has adequately treated all parts of the world and all natures heavenly, angelic, and corruptible, it remains for us (if we are mindful of our promise) to interpret the whole passage again in relation to man, and to prove by the facts themselves that every mode of speech in the whole work includes such hidden senses and deep truths about human nature as it does about the three worlds treated above. The effort will be no less worthy if in unfolding this fourth exposition we are as diligent as in those above.

How useful and necessary self-knowledge is to man was so demonstrated by Plato in *Alcibiades I*[1] (to pass over the Delphic inscription[2]) that he left nothing new for posterity to try to add on the subject. Shameless and rash is the study of that man who, still ignorant of himself and not yet knowing whether he is able to know anything, nevertheless boldly aims at a knowledge of things remote from him.

Let us turn therefore to ourselves and see (as the Prophet says) how many good things God has made for our souls, so that, in consequence of giving little heed to understanding ourselves, we may not hear the Father saying in the Canticles, "If thou know not thyself, oh fairest among women, go forth and follow after the steps of the flocks."[3]

You see what penalty awaits us for ignorance. We must leave

---

[1] Plato, *Alcibiades I*, 124a ff.
[2] "Know thyself."
[3] Canticle of Canticles 1:7 (Song of Solomon 1:8).

our Father, and disinheritance follows that departure. What
is more unhappy than this? Likewise we must go forth from
ourselves, for the soul which does see itself is not in itself.
Whoever goes out of himself, however, is violently separated
from himself. What is more bitter than this? In the third place,
we must follow after the steps of our flocks, that is, the steps of
the beasts that are in us, of which we shall speak amply in this
exposition. What is more wretched than this? What is more
vile and contemptible than to become lackeys to the animals
of which nature made us leaders?

Therefore, advancing in the footsteps not of the beasts but
of Moses, let us enter into our very selves, into the inner chambers of the soul, with the Prophet himself opening the way for
us, so that we may successfully recognize in ourselves not only
all the worlds but also our Father and our home.

Chapter One

Before we organize our exposition more elaborately in accordance with the words and order of the Prophet, we must say
some things about human nature in advance and, incidentally,
explain some terms, so that the meaning of the whole may
thereafter be more clearly understood.

Man consists of a body and a rational soul. The rational soul
is called heaven, for Aristotle calls the heaven a self-moving
living being, and our soul (as the Platonists prove) is a self-
moving substance.[4] Heaven is a circle, and the soul is also a
circle, or rather, as Plotinus writes, heaven is a circle because
its soul is a circle.[5] Heaven moves in an orbit; a rational soul,
going from causes to effects and returning again from effects
to causes, revolves through an orbit of reasoning. If we were
to explain these things separately to those who have not read
them elsewhere, we should be interpreters not of Moses but of
Aristotle and Plato.

The body is called earth, because it is an earthy and heavy

4 Aristotle, *De caelo* II. 6, 289; Plato, *Phaedrus* 245c.
5 Plotinus, *Enneads* IV. 4. 45.

substance. Made from dirt *(humus)*, as Moses writes, it gave its name to man *(homo)*. But between the earthly body and the heavenly substance of the soul there had to be a connecting link to join together such different natures; to this task was assigned that delicate and airy body which physicians and philosophers call the spirit and which Aristotle says is of diviner nature than the elements and corresponds by analogy to heaven.[6] This is called "light," a term which could not better suit the opinion of physicians and philosophers, who all agree that it is of a very bright substance and that nothing pleases, fosters, and refreshes it more than light.

It may be added that just as every virtue of the heavens (as Avicenna writes) is conveyed to earth by the vehicle of light, so every virtue of the soul, which we have called heaven, every power—life, motion, and sense—joins and is transferred into this earthly body, which we have called earth, through the medium of the luminous spirit.

Let us now come back to the words of the Prophet. We see that heaven and earth were first created, the extremes of our substance, the rational force and the earthly body. When light was finally made, that is, by the addition of the luminous spirit, these were so united that from the evening and the morning, that is, from the nocturnal nature of the body and the morning nature of the soul, was made a single man. Since (as we have shown) every power of life and sense descends to our earth through this light, the earth was truly void and empty before its birth, so that the heaven could not impart the benefits of life and motion to it except through light as a mediator. Therefore, as the cause of the emptiness, Moses at once added that darkness was still upon the earth, since the light had not yet appeared.

Chapter Two

There still remains to be asked the meaning of the expression "and the Spirit of God moved over the waters." Here is pre-

[6] Aristotle, *De spiritu* I, 481.

sented an undifferentiated and universal doctrine of the waters which on the following day is made more specific, when Moses teaches that some are above the heavens and some below. If we wish the true meaning of all of these, let us consult the very nature which our Prophet (as we have often said) faithfully copies and represents.

We saw mention made of three parts of human substance, the rational soul, this mortal body, and the intervening spirit. Two more are left. Between the rational part, by virtue of which we are men, and all that is corporeal in us, whether it be gross or delicate and spiritual, there is an intermediate sensual part which we share with the brutes; and since we share no less with the angels than with the brutes, just as below reason there are the senses through which we have fellowship with the animals, so above reason is the intelligence through which we are able to say with John, "our fellowship is with angels."[7] You see what is below our reason and what is above it. If reason is termed heaven (as we have shown), it is now evident what the super-celestial waters in us are, and likewise the subcelestial ones. The term "waters" suits both parts, the intellectual and the sensual, but for different reasons: the former because it is especially transparent to the rays of divine illumination, the latter because it is amazed and delighted by the transient and perishable. Moses reminds us of this difference when he establishes the latter waters under the heavens, where everything is transient and perishable, and the former above the heavens, where all is directed by pure and eternal intelligence. Therefore when we read of the Spirit of the Lord brooding over the waters on the first day, and the waters are divided into two parts, we should not by any means apply this statement to the waters under the heavens, since above these is borne not the Spirit of the Lord but the heavens.

It remains for the statement to concern those which are above the heavens. Here an important doctrine about the soul is revealed to us. A greater, even divine, intellect illuminates the

7 I John 1:3.

intellect in us, whether it be God (as some would have it) or a mind more nearly related to man's, as almost all the Greeks and Arabs and many of the Hebrews hold. This substance both the Jewish philosophers and Abunasar Alfarabi, in the book which he wrote *On the Beginnings,* called the Spirit of the Lord in explicit terms.[8] It was not without reason that, before Moses had man formed from soul and body through the bond of light, he should mention the bearing of the Spirit over the waters. He did it lest we should by some chance believe this Spirit to be present to our intellect only when it is joined to the body. Moses the Egyptian, Abubacher the Arab,[9] and certain others falsely believed this.

Chapter Three

It remains for us to explain what he means by the gathering into one place of the waters under the heavens, that is, the sensory powers which are below the rational part. This is very obvious, however, to those not wholly ignorant of philosophy. All the sensitive powers flow together like rivers to the sea to what, for this very reason, we call the common sense (if we follow Aristotle, this is in the heart[10]).

It would not be absurd to say that from this sea the five senses of the visible body—hearing, sight, taste, touch, and smell—spread out like five Mediterranean seas to penetrate the continent of the body; this was the avowed opinion of Plato in the *Theaetetus.*[11] Since the perfection of the sensitive powers,

[8] Mohammed ibn Mohammed ibn Tarkhan abu-Nasr al-Farabi, *c.* 870-950, Arabic philosopher of Baghdad and Aleppo. Cf. his *De Intellectu et Intellecto* 392-399 (ed. Gilson, "Archives d'histoire doctrinale et littéraire au moyen âge" [1929], p. 126).

[9] Moses, see above, n. 25, p. 73. Abu-Bakr Mohammed ibn 'Abd-al-Malik ibn Tufail, d. 1186, Moorish physician and philosopher. Cf. here Ibn Baja, *Epistola Expeditionis,* in Munk, *Mélanges de Philosophie Juive et Arabe* (Paris, 1927), pp. 393 ff.

[10] Aristotle, *De anima* III. 2, 425b.

[11] Plato, *Theaetetus* 156a.

which is what we understand by this gathering to their source,
leads to both life and nourishment for the body, which we call
earth; after that gathering of the waters, Moses correctly and
immediately brings in the earth as green and blooming. For the
senses are furnished by nature to all mortals to take care of the
life and health of the body, so that through them, mortals may
know what is harmful to themselves and what is healthful;
then, when these things are known, through the appetite attached to the senses they may reject the former and desire the
latter; finally, through the connected motive power, they may
flee the bad and pursue the useful. The eye sees food, the nos-
trils smell it, the feet approach it, the hands seize it, the palate
tastes it.

We say all this so that we may learn that by the establish-
ment of the waters, that is, of the sensitive powers, abundant
fertility is bestowed upon the earth, which for us has long signified the body.

Chapter Four

But truly, although the rational nature is distinguished by
many powers and potentialities, only its bare substance has
been discussed above. Now we must speak of its adornments and
what I may call its royal furnishings. This is what Moses is
writing of when he says that the sun, moon, and stars were
placed in the firmament. More recent philosophers would perhaps interpret the sun as the active intellect and the moon as
the potential, but since we are in a great controversy with them
on this point, we shall so expound it in the meantime that
wherever the soul turns toward the waters above, toward the
Spirit of the Lord, it shall be called sun, because it becomes
bright all over; wherever it looks at the lower waters, the sensual potentialities from which it contracts some stain of corruption, it shall have the name of moon. The Greek Platonists
would call the sun taken in this way *dianoia* and the moon
doxa, in accordance with the tenets of their doctrine. While we

wander far from our fatherland and live in the night and darkness of this present life, we make most use of the part of us which is turned toward the senses, and hence we believe more than we know. When the day of future life has dawned, we shall be parted from our senses and turned toward more divine things, understanding them by means of another, nobler part. Therefore, it is rightly said that this sun of ours presides over the day and the moon over the night. Likewise, because after having cast off this mortal garment we shall contemplate solely by the light of the sun that which in this wretched night of the body we try to see with all our strength and power rather than do see, the day on that account is bright with the sun alone. The night, on the other hand, drums up and joins to the feeble moon as auxiliaries a host of stars, namely, the powers of combining and dividing, of reasoning and defining, and whatever others there are.

Chapter Five

So much for the cognitive powers of the soul. Now Moses shifts to those whose function is to desire, the seats of anger and wantonness, or lust. These he represents by the beasts and the irrational sort of living things, since they are common to us and the beasts and, what is worse, often drive us to a brutish life. Hence comes that saying of the Chaldeans: "The beasts of the earth dwell in your body."[12] And in Plato's *Republic* we learn that we have various kinds of brutes dwelling within us,[13] so that it is not hard, if it is properly understood, to believe the paradox of the Pythagoreans that wicked men turn into brutes. The brutes are within our bowels, so that we do not have to travel far to pass into them. From this come the fables of Circe and the saying of Theocritus that those whom the goddesses of virtue and wisdom regarded favorably could not be enslaved by the potions of Circe.[14]

---

12 Pico indicates no source for this quotation and gives it only in Latin.
13 Plato, *Republic* 588d. Cf. Eusebius, *Praeparatio evangelica* XII. 46.
14 Theocritus, *Idyllia* IX. 33-36.

Let us see what a variety of brutes the reading of Moses may suggest to us. Some are brought forth from the waters under the heavens, and some from the land. The waters under the heavens, we said, signify the sensual part of man, since it is under the reason and serves it closely. The land is this perishable earthly body itself, by which we are surrounded. Let us consider, therefore, whether some of the desires by which we are motivated pertain more to the body and others to the inner sense which philosophers call the phantasy.

Those which impel us toward food and sex seem to me to look toward the body, for they were given us by God for the care of the body which we feed, and for the procreation of children through whom we may survive when we ourselves are dead. Allured more than is proper by the inducement of pleasure, we abuse these desires, taking care of the flesh, as Paul says, by means of gluttony and lust. It is to be observed that he said not "Make no provision for the flesh" but "Make not provision for its concupiscences."[15] Obviously those desires should be used for necessity, even though not for pleasure; much less should our happiness be based upon them. Let us understand these desires therefore to be meant by the cattle and wild beasts, which are said to be the progeny of the earth rather than of the waters. They are both excited and satisfied by the limbs of this grosser body and were given us by God for its health, although its health is ruined by those who exhaust themselves with drunkenness and destroy themselves with lust.

To the waters, on the other hand, that is, the imaginative sense, we refer those impulses which can be called more spiritual, and the issue of our thought rather than of our flesh. Of this sort are those which urge us to fame, anger, revenge, and the other feelings related to these. These are necessary and useful to those yielding to them in moderation, for one ought to get angry, but within measure, and often revenge is a work of justice, and everyone ought to preserve his dignity and not refuse honors obtained in honest ways. I say this so that even if

15 Romans 13:14.

these beasts which represent the sensual appetites are evil by nature we shall not, like the Manicheans, believe them to have been made by an evil principle rather than by the good God, since God created them and then blessed them. They are all good and necessary to man, but we, becoming excessive in our ambition, rage, anger, and arrogance, make evil by our sin what He who is most good created most good.

Chapter Six

See now how what we have said agrees with what follows, that man was made by God in His own image to have dominion over the fish, the birds, and the beasts, which first the waters and then the land had produced. We have already been discussing man above, but now for the first time we perceive in him the image of God, through which he has power and command over the animals. Man was so constituted by nature that his reason might dominate his senses and that by its law all the madness and craving of anger and lust might be curbed. If the image of God has been blotted out by the stain of sin, we begin to serve the beasts in us, wretchedly and unhappily, and to live among them like the Chaldean king,[16] sinking to the ground, eager for earthly things, forgetting our Fatherland, our Father, His kingdom, and the original dignity given to us as our prerogative. Truly, when man was in a state of honor he did not realize it, but ranked himself with the stupid beasts of burden and became like them.[17]

Chapter Seven

Through the first Adam, who obeyed Satan rather than God and whose sons we all are according to the flesh, we degenerated into beasts, disgracing the form of man. In the newest Adam,

[16] Nebuchadnezzar. Cf. Daniel 4:30.
[17] Psalms 48:13 (King James, 49:12).

however, in Jesus Christ, who fulfilled the will of the Father and with His blood vanquished the sins of the spirit, and Whose sons we all are according to the spirit, we are reformed by grace and regenerated, not as men but as adopted sons of God, so that in us as in Him the prince of darkness and of this world may find nothing.

Fifth Exposition

OF ALL THE WORLDS,
IN SUCCESSIVE ORDER OF DIVISION

Proem to the Fifth Book

As we have shown, in each part of his text Moses discussed the
intellectual, celestial, elemental, and human worlds all at once,
imitating nature, or rather God, the creator of nature, Who
included all of the worlds in each. Nevertheless, following the
same example of nature, which allots to each world its proper
seat, proper rights, and peculiar laws, our Prophet so composed his work by the wonderful and perfect mastery of his art
that, although he discussed all the worlds everywhere in the
same form and with the same veil of words, he assigned individual parts of his work peculiarly to the individual worlds in
successive order. In order to show this, we shall begin to interpret the first part in relation to the first world, the angelic, and
then the other parts in relation to the rest, shrewdly observing
in the words of Moses the golden chain of Homer, and the
rings of Plato depending on the living power of the artificer, as
though on the true stone of the indomitable Hercules.[1]

---

[1] The "stone of Hercules" is an ancient term for lodestone. In Homer,
Zeus speaks of making a golden chain from Olympus to earth, whereby all
things could be drawn upward, though not downward. Plato interprets this
in the *Theaetetus* to mean the linkage of the sun and planetary orbits, by
which all motion is transmitted and preserved. Also in *Ion* 533e ff., Plato
describes the various levels of artistic activity as depending on the Muse
like rings hanging from a magnet. See Homer, *Iliad* VIII. 19-20; Plato,
Theaetetus 153c-d; Eunapius, *Vita Sophist.* (Boiss, p. 7); Marinus, *Vita
Procli* 26; Damascius, acc. Photius, cod. 242.

Chapter One

To speak of the angelic nature, which is pure intellect, let us first imagine that minds are like eyes. What the eye is among corporeal things, the mind is in the spiritual realm. Although the mixture of its own innermost substance includes some light, the eye, in order to perform its task of vision, needs external light, by which to observe the colors and differences of things. Its nature is to see, even though it does not see without the aid of light. The ears and all the other parts of the body, not to speak of inanimate things, are illuminated by the light, but nevertheless do not see. Therefore the eye has received for its lot the power of seeing and has sight by virtue of its own essence, since when it receives light, it can see.

Let us consider the same things on the intellectual level. Intellects are eyes, intelligible truth is light, and the intellect, itself intelligible, has a kind of inner light by which it can see itself but not other things. It needs the forms and ideas of things, like rays of invisible light, for the intelligible truth to be clearly discerned. And it must not be said, as we made clear in the example of the eye, that intellects are not intelligent by nature and, like our souls, have obtained the power of intelligence accidentally. From this arises the theory of those who consider "intellect" an unworthy appellation for God. If we compare the intellect with the eye, which does not see by itself but only with the help of light, then since God is light (for light is truth) and vision is the action in which the eye comes in contact with light, God does not need this step, since He is light itself, as much more remote than the angels are from any ignorance of things as the nature of light is more distant from darkness than the eyes. But let us return to the angels.

The eye, that is, intellectual substance, is not wholly simple; otherwise it could not endure mingling with the oncoming light. From this comes the common doctrine that angels are composed of act and potency, although there is a troublesome dispute as to what the act is, and what the potency, and what their manner of mingling, and also what the Arab Averroes meant when he said that both intellects, the active and the potential, exist in all intellects short of God's. It is enough for us, as far as it concerns us here, for the common opinion to be somehow accepted.

All that we have said, Moses explains to us on the first day. He divides the substance of the angels into heaven and earth, the nature of act and the nature of potency. As the same thing has different properties, however, so also it has different names. Therefore as long as this same act is taken as the virtue bestowing sight on the eye and as the consummation of potency, it is called heaven, because it is, in relation to potency, like heaven to earth. Again, since it is in want of light and cannot by itself perform the proper task of intelligence, it is symbolized by the waters, capable of receiving light but not luminous by their own nature. There is also another ground of likeness in the fact that this actuality is as near to the potency which he calls earth as water is to the earth. But let us turn to the words of the Prophet.

God created heaven and earth, the nature of act and the nature of potency, from which he made the angels. The earth, potency, is void and empty, void of act and empty of light, which it does not receive except through the intervening waters. Since contraries apply to the same subject and it pertains to the same thing to welcome both light and darkness, he added "And darkness was upon the face of the deep." He did not say "upon the land"; the deep, unless we abuse the word, is only the depth of the waters. Upon these waters was borne the Spirit of the Lord, the spirit which is called the Father of Lights by the apostle James,[2] from which the light of intelligible forms soon rises upon them, that is, upon the angelic minds. Perhaps the Saracens understood this too when they said that "the angels were led by God out of darkness into the light and filled

2 James 1:17.

with eternal happiness."[3] A pleasure greater, truer, and more lasting than any other arises from intelligence.

Chapter Two

Next to this world is the heavenly one, whose primary property is to lie between the others, the intelligible one which we have just discussed and the sensible one which we inhabit. We cannot show the essence of any intermediate nature more clearly than by indicating the extremes by which it is bounded, since an intermediate nature is compounded from the extremes. Therefore the Prophet reveals to us his great knowledge of the nature of the heavens when he says that they are placed between the waters and the waters—that is, angelic and corruptible substances—in explanation not so much of their location as of their essence. We have already said that by the waters are understood the forms which are nearest to the potency of earth and which perfect its essence. Just as there is one earth for the angels and another of the elements, since the potency of the two is different, so the explanation of the waters—that is, of the forms—is different on either hand.

The heavens are truly in the middle: from that side comes divine life, from this, corporeality; from that, incorruptible substance, from this, the visible; from that, fixity of essence, from this, change of place; from that, whatever is identical, simple, and uniform, from this, whatever is diverse, complex, and unlike. Thus their lot was assigned by the dispensing providence of the Maker.

Chapter Three

After these considerations Moses reminds us briefly of the purity, placement, and order of the elements, by the gathering of

[3] Pico gives no indication of a particular source for this.

the waters into one place, and by the laws prescribed to the sea lest it overwhelm the land. There are in the elements, besides the tendencies of dull, corporeal nature, laws imposed by the intelligent cause by which they are ruled and held in their places. Nothing can show this better than the restraints upon the waters, by which the ocean, whose fury would carry it around the whole sphere of the earth just as the whole sphere of fire rests upon the whole of the air, is held back in check as if admonished by the teacher's rod and comes no farther than our safety and the life of all living things demand. This cannot be attributed to the necessity of matter, which inclines all the elements alike to the shape of spheres; nor to the fortuitous collision of atoms, as Epicurus dreams; nor to the seminal power of a dumb nature unaware of any end, as Strato says;[4] but to a final cause alone, to aim at which is the property only of mind and intellectual foresight.

Therefore it comes about that Moses, about to treat of the order of the elements, mentions this alone, and that this strong argument for the power and wisdom of God was so often brought forward by the prophets. From this come the statements in Proverbs that "with a certain law and compass God enclosed the depths," and that "He compassed the sea with its bounds";[5] and in Jeremiah, "Will not you then fear me, saith the Lord, Me who have set the sand a bound for the sea";[6] and also "Thou hast set a bound which the waters shall not pass over nor overwhelm."[7] Since the whole disposition of the elements was designed especially for those compound things which are alive, God at once after the fundamental ordering of the earth and the waters gave commands to the earth to bring forth plants. Otherwise the treatment of this work relates to the fifth day.

4 Strato of Lampsacus, d. c. 270 B.C., head of the Peripatetic school after Theophrastus. Cf. Cicero, *Academica* II. 121; *De natura deorum* I. 35.
5 Proverbs 8:27, 29.
6 Jeremiah 5:22.
7 Psalms 103:9.

Chapter Four

After discussing the celestial and elemental spheres, and thus the whole of the physical universe, it remained for Moses to speak of the inhabitants and citizens of this universal city, not only those in the heavens, whom he had to discuss first, as though the senate and prefects of the city, as it were, but also those on earth, as though the plebeians and the people.

Therefore he first mentions the heavenly bodies, which God placed in the firmament to be for signs and seasons, to shine in the sky, and to give light upon the earth: I mean the sun, the moon, and the stars. Very deep questions would have to be handled here, each of which would require a whole volume: How are the stars placed in the firmament? As its more noble parts, as the Peripatetics think, or like the animals in their spheres (fish in the water, cattle on earth), as Eusebius the Mede and Diodorus[8] would have it? This point would require conversation with the astrologers, who, from Moses' statement that God placed the stars for signs, draw support for their science of divining by the stars and of foreknowing future events. This science not only has been sharply criticized by Christians like Basil, who rightly called it a busy deceit,[9] and by Apollinarius, Cyril,[10] and Diodorus, but also was spat upon by the good Peripatetics. Aristotle despised it and, what is more, according to Theodoretus,[11] it was repudiated by Pythagoras and Plato and all the Stoics.

It may perhaps seem to some that we should also inquire here into the nature of the stars, their motion and their governance, and into the spots on the moon and the whole science

---

[8] See above, n. 22, p. 72.

[9] Basil, *Hexaëmeron*, VI. 5-7 (Migne, *P.G.*, XXIX, 128 ff.). Cf. Eusebius, *Praeparatio evangelica* VI. 11 (Migne, *P.G.*, XXI, 477a-480a).

[10] Apollinarius the Younger, see n. 22, p. 72. Cyril, 376-444, saint, bishop of Alexandria; cf. his *Homilia Paschales* (Migne, *P.G.*, LXVII, 721c-724a).

[11] Theodoretus, *De Providentia* 5 (Migne, *P.G.*, LXXXI, 624).

of astronomy. But if we stoop to these topics, although they are beautiful and worth knowing, we shall perhaps hear the saying of Horace, "But now was not the time for this."[12] Therefore we put them off for the projected work in which, reconciling Aristotle to Plato, we have undertaken to discuss and examine the whole of philosophy to the best of our ability.

Chapter Five

Therefore let us come back to Moses, who, after speaking of the heavenly animals, mentions in proper order the earthly ones which dwell in the water, on land, or in the air, if the birds can be said to dwell in the air. Let no one here expect or demand from us a discussion of how the bodies of animals are generated from the elements, or how seminal reasons are imposed on things by God, or whether the life of brutes is drawn from the bosom of their matter, or whether all life arises rather from a divine origin, as asserted by Plotinus,[13] whom, to the public advantage, our friend Marsilio Ficino will soon give us to read in Latin, illuminated by ample comments. The Prophet may perhaps seem to support the latter belief in the place where, after saying "Let the waters bring forth the creeping creature having life," he adds "God created every living creature." Here one should observe, however, that the waters produce at God's command and that God then produces also. Where the work of God is referred to, it is written: "God created every living creature," whereas of the waters is written not "living creature" but "creeping creature having life." It is as if to the waters might be attributed the vehicle of life, that is, the compounded body, but to God, the divine principle, the substance of the soul, which as the giver of life, sense, and motion begins to shine from without on the already constituted body.

But of this at another time. Among the animals of the earth, Moses mentions three: cattle, creeping things, and beasts, by

12 Horace, *Ars poetica* 19.
13 Plotinus, *Enneads* VI; VII. 8.

which he suggests to us three different species of unreasoning brutes and no more. The beasts, which have complete sensory faculties, are allotted a middle place among irrational creatures, since they cannot be taught by man or tamed. The creeping things, which have imperfect senses, are a link between animals and plants. Cattle, which though destitute of reason are nevertheless susceptible in some measure to human training, seem thus to participate in reason somewhat, and are allotted a middle position between brutes and men.

Chapter Six

Thus far we have dealt with three worlds: the supercelestial, the celestial, and the sublunary. Now we must deal with man, of whom it is written, "Let us make man to our image." Man is not so much a fourth world, like some new creature, as he is the bond and union of the three already described. There is, however, a custom often practiced by the kings and princes of the earth, when they have founded magnificent and noble cities, of placing in the center of them statues of themselves to be looked at and seen by all. God, the sovereign of all things, did the same when after constructing all the machinery of the world He last of all placed man in the midst of it, formed to his own image and likeness.

It is a difficult question why man has this privilege of being in the image of God. If we reject the folly of Melito,[14] who represented God in human form, and revert to the nature of reason and mind, which like God is intelligent, invisible, and incorporeal, we shall prove that man is like God, especially in that part of his soul which displays the image of the Trinity. But let us recognize that as in the angels these same things are much stronger and less mixed with the opposite nature than in us, the angels have more likeness and affinity with the divine nature.

[14] A saint; bishop of Sardis in the 2nd century. There is some question whether he actually held these views, although they are attributed to him by Origen.

We seek something peculiar to man in which we may ascertain both the dignity proper to him and the image of the divine substance which he shares with no other creature. What can it be but the substance of man which (as some Greek commentators intimate) encompasses by its very essence the substances of all natures and the fullness of the whole universe? I say by its very essence, moreover, because not only the angels, but any intelligent creatures whatever include all things in themselves in some degree when, filled with their forms and reasons, they know them.

Truly, just as God is God not only because He understands all things, but because in Himself He assembles and unites the total perfection of the true substance of things, so also man (although differently, as we shall show, else he would be not the image of God, but God) collects and joins to the completeness of his substance all the natures of the world.

We cannot say this of any other creature, angelic, heavenly, or sensible. The difference between God and man is that God contains all things in Himself as their origin, and man contains all things in himself as their center. Hence in God all things are of better stamp than in themselves, whereas in man inferior things are of nobler mark and the superior are degenerate.

Fire, water, air, and earth in the true peculiarity of their natures exist in this gross, earthly human body which we see. Besides these, there is another, spiritual body more divine than the elements, as Aristotle says, which by analogy corresponds to heaven. There is also in man the life of the plants, performing all the same functions in him as in them—nutrition, growth, and reproduction. There is the sense of the brutes, inner and outer; there is the soul, powerful in its heavenly reason; there is participation in the angelic mind. There is the truly divine, simultaneous possession of all these natures flowing together into one, so that we may exclaim with Mercury,[15] "A great miracle, oh Asclepius, is man!"[16]

Human nature can take its greatest glory in this name, be-

[15] Mercury, Hermes Trismegistus, or the Egyptian god Thoth, reputed author of writings on occultism and theology of the first three centuries A.D.
[16] *Asclepius* I. 6 (*Hermetica*, ed. W. Scott, I, 294).

cause of which no created substance disdains to serve it. The earth, the elements, and the beasts wait upon it as its servants, the heavens labor for it, and the angelic minds look after its salvation and beatitude, if what Paul writes is true, that all ministering spirits are sent to minister to those who are destined for salvation as their inheritance.[17] It ought not to seem wonderful to anyone that all creatures should love the one in whom they all recognize something of themselves, nay, even their entire selves with all their qualities.

Chapter Seven

Earthly things are subject to man and the heavenly bodies befriend him, since he is the bond and link between heaven and earth; but they cannot both have peace with him unless he who in himself sanctifies their peace and alliance is at peace with himself. But let us beware, I pray, that we do not misunderstand the greatness of the honor we have been given. Let us always hold it in our mind's eye as a sure, proven, and indubitable truth that just as all things favor us when we keep the law which has been given to us, so if through sin or evasion of the law we forsake the beaten path, they will all be unfriendly, hostile, and dangerous. It is reasonable that to the same extent that we do injury not only to ourselves but also to the universe, which we encompass within us, and to almighty God, the creator of the world itself, we should also experience all things in the world as the most severe punishers and powerful avengers of injuries, with God among the foremost. Therefore let us dread the penalties and torments which await the transgressors of divine law. It is these who, as the oracle said, δαίμονες οἱ ψοιτῶσι περὶ χθόνα καὶ περὶ ποντον ἀκάματοι δαμνανται ὑπαὶ μάστιγι θεοῖο, that is, who hurry about the land and sea, and when exhausted are subdued by the scourge of God. It is these whom the heavens, the earth, and all the unshakable justice of the universal commonwealth pursue and strike with lightning.

[17] Hebrews 1:14.

Indeed, they are guilty of outraging the universe and insulting the divine majesty, whose image they have defiled with the filthy stain of their iniquity. Thus perhaps it comes about that in the prophets, when any command or prohibition is proclaimed by God, heaven and earth are called as witnesses, because the transgression of the command injures them also, and as long as they serve God they will approve the punishment of the wicked for the affront suffered by both. It surpasses all folly for us to believe that a citizen honored with the highest rank may be permitted to transgress with impunity against the prince and the universal commonwealth, which deserve the best from him, and not be given over at once to the lictors and the executioner to be racked and tortured, or buried alive with stones by the consent of the whole people. There are hangmen and lictors in this commonwealth of God, evil demons sentenced to this basest of professions as punishment for their ancient sins. Hence Paul said "I delivered him to Satan for the destruction of the flesh."[18]

From this also comes the name of the avenging demon in Orpheus, if by chance we give less credit to our own prophets. Just as every creature hates and abhors the sins of man, so his upright life and behavior is dear and pleasing to all. All the things which are included in man and connected with him by so close a bond cannot be excluded from participation in his good and evil. Hence comes the saying in the gospel, "If a sinner has repented, all the angels rejoice in gladness,"[19] and thus is made apparent the plan of that mystery which was hidden for centuries, that our nature, corrupted in the first Adam and defiled by his fall, should be redeemed through the cross of Christ.

For our sake the son of God was made man and was nailed to the cross. It was fitting that He who is the image of the invisible God, the first-born of all creation, and on whom all things were founded, should be joined in ineffable union to him who was made in the image of God, who is the link of all

18 I Corinthians 5:5.
19 Luke 15:10.

creation, and in whom all things are encompassed. If all nature was endangered along with man, his fall was not to be overlooked, nor could it be retrieved by any but Him through whom all nature was established.

Sixth Exposition

OF THE AFFINITY OF THE WORLDS
WITH EACH OTHER AND
WITH ALL THINGS

Proem to the Sixth Book

God is unity so distinguished in three aspects that He does not lose the simplicity of unity. There are many signs of the Holy Trinity in the creation. We shall here take up only one of these, which as far as I know has not hitherto been brought up by anyone: the fact that the unity which we see in creatures is of three different modes. First, there is that unity in things whereby each is one to itself, remains the same as itself, and is in harmony with itself. Secondly, there is that through which one creature is united to another and through which all parts of the world are ultimately one world. The third and most important of all is that whereby the whole universe is one with its Maker, as an army is with its leader. This threefold unity is present in each thing through its own single and simple unity derived from that One which is both the first one and at the same time three and one, the Father and the Son and the Holy Spirit. The power of the Father, creating everything, distributes his own unity to all; the wisdom of the Son, setting all in order, unites them and ties them together; and the love of the Spirit, turning everything toward God, attaches the whole work to its Maker by the bond of charity.

As God is more close to us, so he is more one with us than we are with ourselves. On the other hand, each thing is more closely joined to itself than to other parts of the world. Instructed thus in the order of universal charity, if we wish to follow the divine law written on the tablets of nature, we should first love God Himself above ourselves and all else, in the second place ourselves, and in the third, our neighbors.

Our Prophet said enough of that unity by which each thing is one to itself when he examined the nature of all things one by one. That whereby we are united with God will be treated in the next section, where we shall discuss the supreme felicity. There remains that by which the different parts are joined together in a mutual compact, which we shall discuss now.

Chapter One

Now we have seen the natures of things distinguished and placed in their separate stations. Lest we believe that all these were made one universe only because each is contained by each in accordance with its nature, as we showed above, the Prophet also wished to show in his text what ways there are, and how many, in which the natures of things may be joined together, not only calling us to a careful understanding of this, but teaching and demonstrating to us the route and plan by which we can join ourselves to what is best for us. When I considered, before approaching the interpretation of the words, how many ways exist or can be thought of in which things may find an affinity or a bond with each other, and when I ran through all the doctrines of the philosophers on which I have sweated since boyhood, not more than fifteen kinds suggested themselves. These, on turning to Moses, I saw so clearly and appropriately pointed out that I do not believe one can be better instructed in them anywhere else.

Chapter Two

Immediately on the first day, and I do not know whether more briefly or more clearly, he covers five ways in which one thing can be related to another.

Whatever is related to something else is either its essence, or a property of its essence, or is contained in it as a form by a subject, or affects it either by changing what is changed or as an art affects the matter subject to it. In like manner we read in Moses of five comparisons and connections: heaven and earth, the earth and the void, the deep and the darkness, the Spirit of God and the waters, the light and the bodies. Therefore the void and empty earth designates the first type of relation for us, since the earth—that is, matter—is void by its nature unless it is filled with forms from another source.

The darkness on the face of the deep indicates the second relation, for by its own nature the deep is neither light nor dark, but darkness accompanies its nature unless an approaching light puts it to flight; just as the darkness of privation accompanies the formless emptiness of matter until an oncoming form drives it away.

The light appearing in the bodies shows us the third. The light is in them as form is in a subject.

The fourth is shown by heaven and earth, since heaven is not inherent in earth in the way that a form or accident is contained in the thing which it perfects, but is joined to it as an efficient cause to a passive, or as a cause of change to the body which is changed.

An example of the last type of relation is the Spirit of God which moved over the waters. The creative wisdom of the Lord, and the spiritual nature wholly disjoined from traffic with the body, are understood to be joined to bodies only as art, which is in the mind of the architect, is joined to mortar, wood, and stone.

Also consider this order of sequence, that the earth in itself is empty in its native darkness, and then it is joined to the light, and through the light to heaven, and through heaven to spiritual substance. Then let us see how these things are arranged in us. The earth is the earthly body empty of life and devoid of sense, and upon it are darkness, death, torpor, impotence, immobility, insensitivity. The light is life, which animates, arouses, stirs, and moves the body, and provides it with sense. Heaven is the soul, the source of that light, and the Spirit of God

is the intellect, the light of the divine countenance. And this is
more than is necessary of these things now.

Chapter Three

Let us examine what Moses means in the following verses, and
we shall see that he hinted at the other ten ways in which we
may understand the mutual connections of things. Besides the
ones that we have spoken of, there are also those that we shall
now enumerate, since one thing is either a part or an effect
of another. If it is a part, it is either a part inseparable from
its whole, as the sun and the moon and the stars are in the
firmament, or separable, as the parts of the water are from the
whole body of their element, toward which they flow. If it
is an effect, either it springs from an inner seminal reason, as
plants shoot up from the earth, attached and connected to their
parent by natural bonds and ties; or it is made up and composed of its materials, like a mixture of elements, in the way
that the animal bodies are made of water and earth; or it has
an external cause, which can be classified in three ways as
efficient cause, model, or end. We have examples of these three
from Moses, at the time when God creates man, and makes and
creates him with his own image as a model, and the beasts are
under man and are made for the sake of man as for the sake of
an end.

Chapter Four

We have spoken of part and effect and also of whole and cause.
These terms correspond to each other. But we have not completed the kinds of relationship. Of cause there remains that
type of affinity by which a secondary cause obeys and is joined
to a primary, just as when God brings forth, the waters bring
forth, but only as the proximate cause and only as God bids
them, since the primary cause has greater influence than the
secondary.

Likewise there is a secondary end depending on the principal one and connected with it, which Moses wisely indicates by saying that the stars were placed to shine in heaven and give light to the earth. The good of lesser things is not the primary end of heavenly ones. They aim first to shine for themselves, and then afterwards to give light to us too. We read also in Homer that the dawn and the sun rise and bring light first for the immortals and then for mortals.

Beside all these relations, man is related to man and lion to lion, but a lion is neither a part nor an effect of a lion unless it is born of it. The Prophet shows this when he gathers together and unites the fish and the birds and the beasts of the earth.

There is a final type of affinity between the nature of a mean and the extremes. Man resembles man, and animal, animal, because they share the same sort of essence, whether of species or of genus. But the mean is not of the same essence as the extremes, but, somehow compounded from them, it differs from both so that it may communicate with both, Moses indicates this to us when he places the firmament between the waters, dividing the waters above the heavens from the waters below the heavens. Here he adequately displays the nature of the mean, as we stated in the proem of the first book and in Chapter Two of the fifth.

Chapter Five

Let us learn from this also what action we need to be united to better natures, on which depends the whole and highest strength of our felicity. The first day teaches us that, after driving away the night, the light first arose over the waters when the Spirit of the Lord brooded over them. This foreshadows the statement of James that every perfect gift comes from above, from the father of lights.[1] Not to mention the Christians, Jamblichus confirms this when he asserts that human nature

1 James 1:17.

can promise itself little or nothing unless aided by a greater power, a divine one.[2]

If this is true, and acknowledged not only by Christians but by the philosophers, surely all our zeal ought to be so turned toward higher things that we seek strength for our weakness through holy religion, through sacred rites, through vows, and through hymns, prayers, and supplications. Thus the Platonic and Pythagorean discussions began and ended with sacred prayers, and Porphyry, Theodorus, and all the Academics unanimously affirm that nothing is more useful, or indeed necessary, to man.[3] The Indian Brahmans and Persian magi are said never to undertake anything without first offering a prayer.

I introduce these testimonies of the pagans so that those who have been persuaded by an evil demon to believe the pagans rather than the Church may learn even from those on whom they bestow their faith that it is neither ridiculous nor useless nor unworthy of a philosopher to devote great and unremitting care to holy prayers, rites, vows, and hymns jointly sung to God. If this is helpful and proper for the human race, it is especially useful and proper for those who have given themselves up to the study of letters and the life of contemplation. For them nothing is more necessary than to purify by an upright life those eyes of the mind which they turn repeatedly toward the divine, and to enlighten them more amply with the light obtained from above through the use of prayer and, mindful always of their own weakness, to say with the Apostle, "Our sufficiency is from God."[4]

Chapter Six

Let us examine again what the disposition of the water and the land teaches us. Let us learn from the land that we shall

---

2 Jamblichus, *De Mysteriis Aegyptiorum* II. 11; V, L4.

3 It is not certain here to which Theodorus Pico refers. Porphyry, *Ad Marcellam* 18; Augustine, *De civitate Dei* X. 9.

4 II Corinthians 3:5.

not bear the fruit with which we are pregnant unless we check
and drive back the onslaught of the fleeting and perishable
matter assailing us and thrust away from our bodies the whirl-
pools and torrents of pleasure rushing upon us like water. Let
us learn from the waters that they were not thought suitable
for producing fish until they were collected into a single complete unity of their whole element. Neither shall we be able to
bring to light any progeny worthy of our divinity if we have
been distracted and turned aside to other things, and if, having
collected all our strength, we are not carried forward by a
single-minded purpose. There is also contained here this deeper
mystery: just as it is plainly the final happiness of drops of
water to reach the ocean, which is the fullness of the waters;
so for our happiness, whatever share of intellectual light is in
us must be joined some day to the first intellect and the first
mind of all, which is the fullness and totality of all understanding.

Chapter Seven

But the most important thing is what the doctrine of the firmament shows us, that the lower waters cannot be enriched by any
gift from the upper ones without the intervention of the heavens between them. Let us therefore keep it in mind that the
coupling of the extremes can be brought about only through
that nature which, as the mean between them embracing both,
unites them suitably with each other, because it has already
united them together in itself through the peculiarity of its
own nature.

Let this remind us of the great sacrament which is foolishness
to the heathen, a scandal to the Hebrews, and the goodness and
wisdom of God to us: that man can be united to God only
through Him Who, since in Himself He united man to God,
can, as a true mediator, so attach men to God that just as in
Him the Son of God put on manhood, so through Him men
are made sons of God. If what we say is true, that the extremes
can be joined together only through the mean; and if that is

truly to be called a mean which has already united the extremes in itself; and if that ineffable dispensation by which the Word is made flesh occurs only in Christ; then it is through Christ alone that the flesh can ascend to the Word, and there is not (as John truly wrote) any other name under heaven through which it is necessary for men to be saved.[5] Let them diligently give heed to this, who, when they say they believe in Christ, nevertheless believe that the common religion, or for each man that in which he was born, is enough for achieving felicity. Let them not believe me, nor the arguments themselves, but John and Paul and Christ Himself, who said "I am the way; I am the door; and whoever does not enter through me is a thief and a robber."[6]

5 John 20:31.
6 John 14:6.

Seventh Exposition

OF THE FELICITY
WHICH IS ETERNAL LIFE

Proem of the Seventh Book

If, with the completion of the sixth exposition, we have discussed the levels, order, and nature of the whole world as though in six days, it remains for us in this seventh treatise, like the sabbath of our commentary, to treat of the sabbath of the world and of the repose—that is, the felicity—of the creatures whose nature we established in the preceding treatises; or, to speak more accurately, it remains for us to listen to Moses speaking as a true seer of all future things.

There is, as the theologians assert, one felicity which we can attain through nature and another which we can attain through grace. The former they call natural, the latter supernatural. Of the first, the natural, Moses has said enough, since having learned the nature of things we know their natural felicity also. It remains, therefore, for Moses to teach us about the second, showing himself a prophet rather than a doctor, since when he wrote, grace did not yet exist, although it was to exist in the future.

But since I seem to see certain scholars—or should I rather say good-for-nothings and idlers who call themselves philosophers, when there is nothing which they are less—straightaway laughing at both grace and supernatural felicity as though they were empty names and old wives' tales, I have decided as a proem to the seventh book to hold a very brief disputation with them on this point. It will be useful to everybody individually and is exceedingly necessary to the work which we have undertaken, in which we are proving that the opinion of the the-

147

ologians is clearly supported and established by the deepest roots of philosophy.

Felicity I define as the return of each thing to its beginning. For felicity is the highest good, and the highest good is what all things seek; what all things, however, seek is that which is the beginning of all things, as Alexander of Aphrodisias, in his commentary of the first philosophy,[1] and the Greek interpreters of Aristotle's *Ethics* all confirm. Therefore the end of all things is the same as the beginning of all: one God, omnipotent and blessed, the best of all things which can exist or be thought of; hence the two appellations used by the Pythagoreans, One and Good. He is called one since He is the beginning of all things, just as unity is the beginning of all numbers, and good since He is the end, rest, and absolute felicity of all things. Now we can see, if we are a little more clever, the basis of the double felicity. Felicity is the possession and attainment of this primal good. Created things can acquire this good in two ways, either in themselves or in itself. In itself, this good is exalted above all things, inhabiting the heights of its own divinity; in all things, it is found diffused, here more perfectly and there less so, according to the nature of the things which participate in it.

Therefore, as the poets write, Jove is whatever you see, and all things are full of Jove.[2] Since each nature has God within it in some way, since it has as much of God as it has of goodness (and all things which God made are good), it remains for it, when it has perfected its own nature in all parts and has attained its potential, to attain God also within itself; and if the attainment of God is felicity, as we have shown, it is in some way happy in itself. This is the natural felicity, of which more or less is allotted to different things according to the diversity of their natures. Fire is a thing lacking soul, but it participates in God in many ways. In the first place it exists, and everything

---

1 Alexander of Aphrodisias, *In metaphysicam commentaria,* ed. Hayduck, p. 820, lines 25 ff.

2 Virgil, *Eclogue* II. 60. Cf. Augustine, *De civitate Dei* IV. 9-10 (*P.L.,* XLI, 119); Albertus Magnus, *Commentaria de causis,* lib. I, t. IV, c. V; *Summa de creaturis,* II, q. 5, a. 2.

which is, exists through participation in God, Who is being itself. Moreover, insofar as fire is a definite species and actuality, it is like God, who is the first species and the first actuality. When fire produces fire, it imitates in proportion to its nature the divine creativity; when it contains itself within the bounds of its sphere, justice; and when it serves us, benevolence. When fire does these things, it has attained its perfection, and is happy to the extent that it is capable of happiness. More happy are the plants, which also have life; and happier still are the animals, which have been allotted consciousness, so that the more perfection they have, the more divinity they find within themselves.

In the best condition of all mortal things is man, who excels the others in natural felicity as in nature, being possessed of those extraordinary endowments greatly conducive to felicity, intelligence and freedom of choice. Highest among creatures is the angelic mind, because of the nobility of its substance and its attainment of its end, in which it participates in the highest degree because it is close to it and joined to it. But indeed, as we said above, through *this* felicity neither plants nor animals nor men nor angels attain God, who is the highest good, in God Himself, but only in themselves.

Therefore the degree of felicity gradually changes according to the capacities of different natures. For this reason the philosophers who have spoken only of *this* felicity have placed that of each thing in the best working of its own nature. In fact, even to the angels, whom they call minds and intellects, and whose supreme perfection they acknowledge because the angels understand God, they ascribe no further knowledge of God than that by which angels know themselves, so that the angels understand God only so far as His nature is made manifest in their own substance. In regard to man, although different philosophers hold different opinions, nevertheless all have kept within the narrow bounds of human capacity, limiting the felicity of man either to the mere search for truth, as the Academics do, or to its attainment through the study of philosophy, as Alfarabi said.

Avicenna, Averroes, Abu Bakr, Alexander, and the Platonists seem to allow somewhat more, basing our reason, as on its proper end, on the active intellect or on some greater one which is nevertheless related to us; but they lead man neither to his beginning nor to his end. I neither reject nor despise their arguments and opinions, if they are taken as speaking only of natural felicity. But it is certain that through this, neither men nor angels can be exalted any more highly than they say.

This is strongly confirmed by the fact that since nothing can rise above itself by relying on its own strength (otherwise it would be stronger than itself), so nothing relying on itself can attain a felicity any greater or more perfect than its own nature. But if only this felicity exists in things, let the philosophers tell me why they themselves acknowledge that among the animals, only man was born for felicity. Although other things beside man also reach their ends, we can say that their felicity is less than man's; but how shall we defend the proposition that it does not exist? Moreover, since the things below man never exceed the bounds established by nature, and man almost always does, the human condition, unless it boasts of some other privilege, seems the least happy of all. Therefore, I pray, let us listen to the holy theologians reminding us of our dignity and of the divine goods freely promised us by the most generous of fathers, lest, cruel to our own souls and ungrateful to God the creator, we reject them. We said above that the highest felicity lies in the attainment of God, who is the highest good and the beginning of all things; also, that this attainment can be achieved in two ways, since we reach God either in the creatures in which he participates or in himself. We have shown, and we shall show, that through their own powers, created things cannot achieve this ultimate felicity, but only the former. The former, if we look closely, is rather the shadow of felicity than true felicity, just as the creature through which you touch God is not the highest good, but a meager shadow of that divine and highest good.

Let it be added that through the former felicity, things are restored to themselves rather than to God, not achieving a return to their beginning, but only avoiding a departure from themselves. The true and perfect felicity, however, carries us back to the contemplation of the face of God, which is the whole of the good, as He himself said, and leads us to perfect union with the beginning from which we sprang. The angels can be raised to this, but they cannot ascend to it; thus Lucifer sinned in saying "I will ascend into heaven."[3] To this level man cannot go, but can be drawn; therefore Christ, who is felicity itself, said: "No man comes to me unless my Father has drawn him."[4] The brutes and things below man can neither go nor be drawn to that level.

Therefore only men and angels are made for that felicity which is the true felicity. Vapor can rise upwards, but not unless drawn by the rays of the sun; stone and all heavy substances can neither receive the rays to so great an extent nor be carried up by them. These rays, this divine power, this influence, we call grace, since it makes men and angels pleasing to God.

The philosophers have a clear example of this doctrine in bodies. Some bodies are borne in a straight line and some in a circle. The linear motion, by which the elements are carried to their proper places, stands for the felicity through which things are established in the perfection of their own nature. Circular motion, through which a body is carried around to the point from which it started, is the most express image of the true felicity, through which a creature returns to the beginning from which it proceeded.

See how everything corresponds on both sides. Bodies do not move in circles unless they are immortal and incorruptible. No substance returns to God except the immortal and eternal. The elements, to perfect their motions, need no other force than the impulse of levity or gravity imposed on them at creation, just as individual things are brought to their natural felicity by their own proper impetus and force. But the heavenly bodies, although adapted to circular motion, are not in themselves sufficient to perform this motion, but need the divine

3 Isaiah 14:13.
4 John 6:44.

mover to turn and revolve them. They are suited to perpetual
revolution only insofar as they can receive it, not produce it.

It is no different for us and the angels. Our nature is such that
we cannot go in a circle and come back upon ourselves, but we
can be moved in a circle and brought back to God by the motive
power of grace. Hence comes that saying, "Whosoever are led
by the Spirit of God, they are the sons of God."[5] "Who are led,"
it says, not "who move." We differ from the heavens in that
they are moved by the necessity of their nature and we in proportion to our freedom. The moving spirit knocks unremit-
tingly at the door of your soul. If you fail to hear, you will be
left wretched and unhappy in your own torpor and weakness.
If you let it in, you will be carried back at once, full of God,
along the orbit of religion to the Father, to the Lord, to possess
life forever in him, in whom you always had life even before
you were made. This is the true felicity, to be one spirit with
God, so that we possess God in God, not in ourselves, knowing
him just as we are known. For he knows us not in ourselves, but
in himself. Likewise we shall know him in himself and not in
ourselves. This is our whole reward, this is the eternal life, this
is the wisdom which the wise men of this world do not know,
that from every imperfection of multiplicity we are brought
back to unity by an indissoluble bond with him who is himself
the One.

For this felicity Christ prayed to his Father in this fashion:
"Father, bring it about that just as you and I are one, they also
may be one in us."[6] This is what Paul was hoping for when he
said, "I shall know Him not in part, but as He is."[7] And if he
hoped, did he not say rightly, "Who shall separate me from the
love of Christ?"[8] And he wished to be dissolved, that he might
become one with Christ. From this felicity fell the devil, because he wished to climb up to it, not to be carried, and so he
lost what he would have had if he had remained. On this basis
we know the fate of infants who die unbaptized; they remain

5 Romans 8:14.
6 John 17:21.
7 I Corinthians 13:12.
8 Romans 8:35.

as they were, neither stripped of their own goods nor enriched by divine ones.

We must fall into one of two divisions, either the deepest misery or the highest happiness. He who is responsible for not receiving the moving spirit not only makes himself immune to grace but also defiles his own nature, whose health requires him to seek the spirit once he has recognized it, and not to reject it; and without doubt the nature which rejects or despises the hope of a greater possible good cannot be right. Therefore whoever does not put his faith in Christ after recognizing Him is rightly deprived not only of the first felicity, but also of the second, the natural, since it is only a corrupt and fallen nature that does not desire grace.

Just as we who live under the Gospel accept Christ as the power and wisdom of God, loving and holding fast to him as already given to the human race, so the patriarchs under the old law accepted him when they believed assuredly in his future coming and eagerly hoped for it and ardently desired it. But just as they accepted him not as already present but as yet to come, so they did not enjoy the fruit of the indwelling Spirit in the present until after he came. Then after the ineffable sacrifice performed on the altar of the cross, when Christ had come down to them, he swept them to freedom like the moving power of a whirlwind and carried them up to the level of highest felicity. To this felicity religion urges, directs, and impels us, just as we use philosophy as a guide to natural felicity. But if nature is the beginning of grace, so philosophy is the beginning of religion, and there is no philosophy which separates man from religion. Therefore after we have philosophized on nature for six days, it is right for us, at leisure for the divine on the seventh day, to speak with Moses of the supernatural felicity.

Chapter One

As we have shown, two natures are capable of this highest felicity, the angelic and the human. The former is called heaven, the latter earth, since the angels live in heaven and we on earth. Of heaven there is no reason for Moses to say more, since he is writing the law for men, not for angels. Coming down to men, therefore, he says, "The earth was void and empty, and darkness was upon the face of the deep." God does not create a void, and He does not create darkness; but the earth (Moses says) was void, and there was darkness. He does not say that these were created, but that they were.

Why he said this will be clear as soon as we have learned what this void and darkness are. Compared to the angels, human nature, which is called earth, was void from the very beginning, because it sinned at the very beginning. It was void and empty of its original justice, and its face, reason, was shadowed by the darkness of sin. God did not do this, but the malice of man, who willingly deprived himself of the goods with which God had enriched him. Thus the prophet describes the state of our corrupted nature, and in what follows he shows how through Abraham, through himself, through the prophets, and most recently through God's only begotten Son, it will be restored to its pristine dignity and prepared for the highest felicity.

Even at the time when the waters were covered with darkness, stained with the primeval filth of original sin, the Spirit of the Lord brooded over them nonetheless. This is to be understood in two ways. First, men were guided by the light of the divine countenance which is stamped upon us, that is, by the light of natural intelligence. Secondly, the human race at that time was not deserted by the care of divine providence. The Spirit of the Lord brooded over the waters, that Spirit which (as the Apostle says) intercedes for us with unspeakable groanings,[9] and it was considering constantly how to cleanse the waters of the poisons with which the old serpent had stained them; and behold, He at once ordered the light to arise, and the light rose. The wise Abraham was the first founder of the true religion, the first to free himself from the law of nature and to meditate upon the divine law, the first to urge men to worship the one God in opposition to the idols of the gentiles, the first to try to drive

9 Romans 8:26.

away the darkness of error and to declare war upon the evil
demons who are called the princes of darkness; therefore light
is properly synonymous with him. Since all the disciples of the
Lord did this also, the Lord calls them all the light of the world.
This is the first light which shone upon the world and distinguished between the worship of demons and of the true God,
as between light and darkness.

Chapter Two

There followed the law, which is properly called by the name
of firmament, announcing to us at once in its beginning, in this
very passage which we are now discussing, the work of the hands
of God; as David sang, "and the firmament declareth the work
of His hands."[10]

Therefore the Word of God confirmed the law given to
Moses by the angel, which hitherto, more than the greater light,
distinguished the Israelites from the gentiles, that is, piety from
impiety, just as the firmament does the waters above the heavens
from the waters below the heavens.

The Jews are called the waters above the heavens since they
alone, as Jeremiah says,[11] do not fear the signs of heaven,
which the heathen do fear; they alone acknowledge neither stars
nor heaven, but only the Lord and Creator of stars and heaven,
and they honor and worship him whom they have acknowledged. For the opposite reason, the gentiles are the waters under the heavens: they worship and adore the demons dwelling
in the murky air, which is the region above the waters, and
make the visible sky, stars, and planets their gods and lords.

Chapter Three

If some greater strength and the mercy of God had not with-
stood them, the waters which are under the heavens, the serv-

10 Psalms 18:2.
11 Jeremiah 10:2.

ants of idols, would have invaded and occupied the whole
earth. The corruption of the whole world by the first stain de-
manded this, and the authority and power of vengeful Satan
over us required it, guilty as we are of an ancient crime and
liable to such servitude as punishment. But the ever beneficent
and salutary providence of God willed that one part of the
earth, although as meager as the laws of his justice allowed,
should be free from harm from the waters; this is Judea, called
the land of promise, which was promised by God to Abraham
and his posterity.

This interpretation of ours is agreed with by all the prophets,
by whom the frequent assaults of the gentiles on the Israelites
are compared to the incursions of the waters of the sea. Hence
come those verses, "The floods have lifted up their voice"[12] and
"wonderful are the surges of the sea"[13] and "their waters roared
and were troubled"[14] and "we will not fear, when the earth
shall be troubled and the mountains shall be removed into the
heart of the sea."[15] Indeed, the gentiles surrounded Judea, com-
pressed within the confines of a region by no means large,
exactly as the ocean now surrounds on all sides this modest
portion of land which we inhabit. In many places in Christian
literature the gentiles are obviously denoted by waters; for it
is also written "The waters which you have seen are the gentiles";[16] and when the Lord Jesus made wine from water, when
the wine gave out in the house of the Pharisee, you should
imagine, our authors write, that he meant that the waters, that
is, the gentiles, were to be called to the faith that would in the
future be lacking among the Jews, among whom it had formerly
existed. Likewise in secret rites, the tradition is handed down
that water is mixed with the wine because the waters of the
gentiles drink up and absorb the blood of Christ through the
faith of the cross.

12 Psalms 92:3 (King James, 93:3).
13 Psalms 92:4 (King James, 93:4).
14 Psalms 45:4.
15 Psalms 45:3.
16 The Apocalypse (Revelation) 17 15

Therefore that part was delivered from the yoke of the waters by the providence of God so that, even if the rest of the earth should be overwhelmed by the waves of spiritual wickedness and become useless, deserted, and unsuited for the fruits of true religion, there would at least be this. Having received the light which the first day brought forth, and helped in its fertility by the dew of the heavens which were made on the second, that is, by the doctrine of the law, this part would then sprout judgments, ceremonies, and good customs, like grass, plants, and trees, until in the fullness of time it should also sprout with the greatest happiness the very Savior whom Isaiah desired.

Chapter Four

And behold the fullness of time.

For if the number four is the fullness of numbers, will not the fourth day be the fullness of days? See, therefore, what the fourth day brings us. The heavens established on the second day, that is, the law, were without sun, moon, or stars, capable of future brightness, but hitherto dark and not illuminated by any noticeable light.

Then came the fourth day, on which the sun, the lord of the firmament, that is, Christ, the lord of the law, and the moon-like Church, the bride and consort of Christ, and the apostolic doctors who would educate many to justice, like stars in the firmament, began to shine forth for eternity, calling the world to eternal life. The sun did not destroy the firmament, but perfected it, and Christ came not to destroy the law, but to perfect it.

The light of the first day, the pious Abraham, saw the fourth day, which is the day of Christ, and rejoiced. He saw that the rays of his light, of the true religion which he had brought into the world, were to be spread abroad through the whole earth by the sun of justice, the true light illuminating all men. He saw Jesus Christ, the splendor of the Paternal Substance, shining upon those who lingered in the darkness and the shadow of death, and that the prince of darkness, the prince of this world, was cast out and banished from the minds of men. He saw these things and exulted; he saw the fourth day and was glad, this day which the Lord made and in which the Lord was made man, and in which God dwelt among us; let us also exult in it and be glad.

I pray you, Christian brothers, to consider a little more attentively how true and sound the scheme of my interpretation is. Against the stony hearts of the Hebrews it will furnish you with powerful weapons drawn from their own arsenals. In the first place we shall prove from the testimony of the Jews that the works of the fourth day signify the coming of Christ. Secondly, we shall show that nothing represents the Messiah to us more fittingly than the sun, and we shall clearly deduce from the periods of time that the Christ is not still to come in the future but that Jesus of Nazareth, the son of the Virgin, was the Messiah promised to the Hebrews.

It is among the doctrines of ancient Hebrew learning that the six days of Genesis denote the six thousand years of the world, so that what are here called the works of the first day were a prophecy of things to happen in the first millennium of the world; likewise the works of the second of those in the second, and so on, with the same order of succession always kept on both sides. Among the more recent authors this opinion is also confirmed by Moses of Gerona, a theologian of foremost fame among the Hebrews. St. Jerome also mentions it in his exposition of that psalm which is attributed to Moses,[17] and this belief seems to rest especially on the fact that a thousand years, as the prophet says, are one day to God.

Therefore, if this is a true doctrine, the fourth day is a prophecy of what is to happen in the fourth millennium of the world. Now let us show that, according to the annals of the Hebrews and the reckoning of the years which they themselves accept, it was in the fourth millennium of the world that Jesus appeared.

17 Psalms 89 (King James, 90). For Moses of Gerona, see above, n. 25, p. 73.

They count 1556 years from Adam to the deluge and 292 years from the flood to Abraham, and so 1818 years are reckoned from Adam to Abraham.[18] From the birth of Isaac to the fall of the second temple, which was after the death of Christ, they count, in round numbers, about 1660 years. From Isaac to the exodus from Egypt they reckon 430 years; from the exodus to the temple which Solomon built, almost as many; from Solomon to the destruction of the temple by the Babylonians, 410 years; from the rebuilding of the temple under Ezra to its capture by Titus, 420 years.

Thus, if you add all together, you will figure 3508 years from the beginning of the world to Christ, by the thinking of the Hebrews themselves, so that Christ came in the very middle of the fourth millennium. Within the limits of the same millennium, as within those of the fourth day, the light of the moon, the Church, shone upon the whole world, and a countless multitude of martyrs, apostles, and doctors who all became famous within 500 years after the death of Christ illuminated the shadows of our night and the darkness of the firmament, that is, of the law.

But the Hebrews will say, "Granted that Jesus came at this time. You have not yet proved that Jesus was the Christ unless you show that our people believed that the Christ would come at this time." It is a good point, and they ask it justly, and we can easily prove what they rightly ask. There circulate among them as well-understood popular traditions the oracles of Elijah, which say freely and without any symbolism or veil that the Messiah will come in the fourth millennium of the world. Lest these seem made up by me or interpreted arbitrarily, I shall offer the testimony of the very Talmudists with whom our controversy lies, who not only mention these oracles but, with the truth itself compelling them, acknowledge that the time predicted by Elijah for the coming of the Messiah has passed. These words are in the part which is entitled *Aboda Zara,* under the heading *libne edeem: Tana dbe elihau seseth alaphim sana*

18 Pico's figures here actually add up to 1848, which agrees with the total of 3508 in the next paragraph.

haue haolam. Sene alaphim tohu; usne alaphim thora, usne alaphim Jemoth hamas sihi uba hauonothema serabu iashu meon maseias.[19] We interpret these in Latin as follows, translating word for word: "The sons or disciples of Elijah said: six thousand years for the world; two thousand empty, two thousand for the law, and two thousand for the day of the Messiah, and because of our sins, which are many, there have passed those which have passed." So they speak. Now, since with the very words placed before the eyes of all I cannot introduce anything invented or arbitrary, we shall discuss and examine the words of the oracle, and we shall immediately be masters of our purpose.

Six thousand years for the world, it says, which we may interpret in the sense that after the course of six thousand years, as many of our people have believed also, the end of the world is to come like the Sabbath; or if (which is more true) no one knows that day, we may accept it in the sense that nothing in the law is taken as a prophecy of a later time; but this does not pertain to the question proposed. Let us see what follows. Two thousand empty, two thousand for the law, and then the Messiah.

All the Hebrew interpreters say that the oracle calls "empty" the time before God handed down any law to men. But I see a Jew jumping up and saying, "If there are two thousand years before the law and two thousand for the law, then the Messiah was to come not on the fourth day, that is, while the fourth millennium was passing, but rather on the fifth day, after the fourth millennium." But a reply is easy, since undaunted truth provides it. What Elijah said—two thousand empty, two thousand for the law—should not be taken as if the world were to be without law for the whole period of two thousand years, and the law were to endure for two thousand years likewise, but in the sense that the period of natural law would reach the second millennium and the period of the law would reach the fourth. Before the second is over there will come the law, and before the fourth has elapsed, the Messiah.

[19] *Aboda Zara,* 9a. Cf. *Sanhedrin,* 97a; *Zohar,* I, 25a.

I am not inventing or dreaming up this interpretation for myself. Elijah himself teaches it to me, and the Talmudists teach it also. It will soon be clear to you also, Jewish viper, unless you close your ears. Elijah says, "Two thousand empty and two thousand for the law." Let us see in what sense what is said of the emptiness was true, and from that let us learn how to explain what is said of the law. The beginning of the law we take either from Moses or from Abraham. It cannot be taken from Moses because the emptiness would then have lasted over 2300 years, or thereabouts. It is about that many from Adam to Moses. Therefore the begining of the law must be taken from Abraham, to whom was given the covenant of circumcision, the root and foundation of the whole ancient law. From Adam to Abraham, if they consult their own histories, they find that not a complete interval of two thousand years elapsed, but only 1848. Thus it came about that the fullness of the law succeeded the emptiness not after the second millennium but within its limits.

Therefore, for the same reason, the fullness of the gospel had to follow the emptiness of the law not after the fourth millennium but while the fourth was passing. If the Jews continue impudently and stubbornly to deny this, let them listen to their own Talmudists, who strongly support our opinion. They themselves admit that, at the time when they were writing, the time predicted by Elijah for the coming of the Messiah had already passed, and this they impute to their sins. If the words of Elijah were taken in the sense that the Christ was to come after the fourth millennium, not within the limits of the fourth, the Talmudists neither would have nor could have said that the time for the Messiah promised by the prophets had passed, since at the time when the Talmudic doctrine which we have advanced was written, four thousand years since the beginning of the world had not yet passed. According to the Hebrews, as we have shown above, Jesus appeared 3508 years after the beginning of the world. The Jerusalem Talmud, however, as they themselves relate, was written in the three hundredth year after the death of Christ, and the Babylonian a hundred years after

the Jerusalem. Therefore both were composed within the limits
of the fourth millennium, yet both of them admit and lament
that the time predicted by Elijah for the coming of the Christ
has passed.

Where now will they hide themselves, or what hiding-places
will they seek, that they may flee from this sun of ours which
illuminates the universe against their will, and not see it at
all? The Talmudists admit, even if they do not believe the
ancients, that the time predicted by the prophets for the coming of the Christ has passed. They admit that the prophets believed he would come during the time in which they themselves
hold that Jesus came. And their doctors are not wholly un-
truthful when they say that on account of their sins the Messiah
did not come. He did not come for those who did not acknowledge him. He is not the Messiah, the Redeemer of the worst
captivity, the beneficent King, the restorer of the land of the
promise, the heavenly Jerusalem, except to those who have
owned him as the Messiah. If in his own land his people did not
receive him when he came, they are no longer his who were his;
but from east and from west come those who will rest in the
bosom of Abraham, while the chosen people are cast into outer
darkness.

Thus is solved the troublesome problem that the Messiah was
to be for the salvation of the Hebrews, but that Christ was their
ruin. Those are not Hebrews who do not follow and cherish
the King and Lord promised the Hebrews from the stock of
David, but who rather, with every outrage and insult, fasten
him like a robber, blasphemer, and profaner of the temple, to
the cross. If they were sons of Abraham, they would stand firm
in the practices of Abraham and receive joyfully the coming of
this day, the fourth, which Abraham enjoyed in anticipation.

The Messiah brought peace for men, but not for all. The
angels did not say simply "and on earth peace to men," but
added "to men of good will."[20] The same sun which gives light
to pure eyes darkens and blinds the weak and feeble, and it is
with good reason that He who is Savior to the good is hurtful

20 Luke 2:14.

to the wicked, and He who gladdens his friends with his power and favor, hurls lightning at his enemies and ruins them. If evil had come to the Jews from accepting Christ, he would not have been Christ. But if evil came from crucifying him, he was certainly Christ, who, even when he was nailed to the cross and appeared wholly conquered, triumphed over his conquerors in such an overthrow and disaster for them.

Therefore why do you wait for the sun, you blind ones? The sun is here and shines, but it shines in darkness,[21] and your darkness does not comprehend it. The fourth day has passed, when the sun rose which has not destroyed the law but has perfected it, just as the sun does not demolish the firmament but adorns, perfects, and brightens it. We have proved from the order of the fourth day and from the time of Christ's coming that what is said here ought to be understood in relation to him. Let us prove the same thing from a similarity of metaphor, since we can picture Christ by nothing more fitting than the sun. He placed his tabernacle in the sun, and he sprang from the tribe of Judah, whose emblem is the lion, the animal of the sun, and when Plato in the *Republic* calls the sun the visible son of God,[22] why may we not understand it as the image of the invisible Son? If he is the true light illuminating all minds, does he not have as his most exact likeness the sun, which is the light of the senses illuminating all bodies? But why do we look for anything else? Let us ask the sun itself, which, eclipsed behind the moon during Christ's passion, clearly showed us the accordance of its nature.

With the best right, not to touch on any loftier reason, the day which the astrologers call the sun's we have called the Lord's day, and have surrendered it wholly to his worship. We have also shown that there is no further reason for us to worship the physical sun (as the gentiles once did) as king and lord of the sky, now that the invisible sun, coeternal and coequal with the Father, by Whom both heaven and earth were made, has brought light to men, who were sitting in the shadow of death.

21 John 1:5.
22 Plato, *Republic* VI, 508e.

Chapter Five

Now let us consider whether the works which follow the fourth day correspond to what is known to have happened after the coming of Christ, so that we may finally, when we have learned that everything confirms and agrees with this interpretation of ours, accept it as true and established. Let us see what is done after the fourth day. The waters bring forth fish and birds; the land brings forth cattle and beasts of burden. Let us recall to mind that which, we said above, is signified by the waters that, located under the heavens, were gathered into one place; and likewise by the land, which was made immune from floods. We said that the gentiles are represented by the waters and the Israelites by the land, and we proved this with much evidence from the prophets and by patterns of resemblance. We saw that before the rising of the sun, the sterile waters produced nothing of value; the land, indeed, was productive, but only of poor crops and herbs and grass. After the creation of the sun the waters, with greater fertility than the land, bring forth two kinds of living things: birds and fish. The land, no longer content with trees and shrubs, produces great herds of cattle and beasts of burden. Do you not see, even if I keep silent, the fulfillment of the prophecy of the good Simeon that this sun of ours should be a light to the revelation of the gentiles and the glory of thy people, Israel?[23] Do we not have clearly before our eyes, if we interpret nothing otherwise, both the calling of the gentiles, and the transformation of the earthly Jerusalem and the shadowy synagogue into the true Church and the eternal and heavenly city of God? Before the rising of the sun the waters produce nothing. The land produces only sparsely and scantily. This is so because there was no form of life among the gentiles before the coming of Christ, no fruit of the true religion.

Among the Israelites there was indeed some hope, and they

[23] Luke 2:32.

knew in part the path of light and cherished the true religion, but in a primitive and imperfect form until He came who is the way, the truth, and the life. And unless we revert to this mystery, let someone show me the reason why the ornaments and progeny of the earth were divided so that it brought forth some before making of the sun and some afterwards. Likewise why do the waters produce nothing before the sun, while the land produces something? Why are two kinds of living things produced by the waters and only one by the land? Why are the birds, animals of the air, assigned to the waters?

To discuss the first question, it is not enough to say, like some, that the plants and grasses were produced from the earth before the making of the sun so that they might not seem created by its power. By the same reasoning, the fish and birds and the splendid array of the elements ought also to have been created before the sun, lest their making be credited to its power. Moses would then have left a doubt that even though the light of the sun might not have been necessary for producing imperfect things like plants, it nevertheless was needed for producing animals, which are more perfect. Consequently, if the more perfect things might have come to light without its help, the less perfect could have been made without it also. The proposition cannot be converted, however, so that if the less noble things like plants, the lowest class of living things, had been made without it, all kinds of animal natures could also have been produced without the intervention of its work.

The plan of the author is discovered more correctly, therefore, from what we have said. Likewise, if anyone says that animals which live in the waters have been attributed to the waters, he will see rather that only one kind should have been attributed to them, and two to the land. Land rather than water is the home of the birds, and without any question, if we consider the nature of the animal, a bird is an animal of land or air, in no way aquatic.

But listen to the most profound reasons of all drawing us, even against our wills, to the mysteries of Christ and the Church. Surely if all things agree with the truth, as Aristotle says, all things ought to agree with Christ, who is the truth itself. Not without reason, nor for nothing, did He say so often to the Hebrews, "Search the Scriptures; the same are they that give testimony of me";[24] and He maintained that many things, even all things, were predicted of him in the law, the psalms, and the prophets.

Often we become blind from too much light, and unless He takes the veil from our eyes, we cannot look closely at the wonders of his law. With his help let us come to the revelation of the mysteries and symbols. Two kinds of animals are produced from the waters and one from the land because there was a greater number of believers among the gentiles than among the Jews. The land, however, produces more perfect animals than the waters, even though less numerous, namely, the beasts of burden and all the quadrupeds. Although more gentiles than Hebrews believed, the more perfect believers were Hebrews, from whom came the Apostolic founders of the whole religion.

Likewise the water brings forth two different species, birds and fish, but the land only one, since among the gentiles some are brought to Christ from the service of demons and others from the law of nature. Every Hebrew is a Hebrew only insofar as he is not permitted to live within the bounds of nature, since God has given him a peculiar law not common to other peoples. God did not deal alike with all nations and did not manifest his judgments to them all. Therefore the fish signify those who have come to us from the worship of demons, not only because the waters, as we showed above, represent the impiety of the gentiles, but because, as Jonathan the Chaldean attests, evil demons are often represented in the Holy Scriptures by animals which live in the waters.

The birds signify those who are brought to grace from the customs of nature. The reason for this is clear from what we wrote at great length about natural and supernatural felicity in the proem to this book. We showed the heavens to be the most express image of supernatural felicity, and natural felicity to be secondary and imaginary rather than true.

24 John 5:39.

Therefore those who pursue this, using the laws of nature, are fitly denoted by birds, inhabitants not of the first and true heaven, but of the air, which for a secondary and imaginary reason also claims for itself the name of heaven; for this reason birds are often called birds of heaven in the Holy Scriptures.

See with what deep wisdom the birds are attributed not to the air but to the water. Those who lived according to nature, like Socrates, perhaps, and most of the philosophers, were considered gentiles also, since they called themselves gentiles and lived among the gentiles. Therefore both species are jointly assigned to the water. How well this interpretation agrees with the evangelical and apostolic doctrines is easy to show. Paul represents the Apostles converted from the Hebrews as oxen,[25] beasts of the land, and so do our doctors of the Gospel, in the place where the merchants are driven from the temple,[26] and Christ calls the Israelites sheep. The Apostles to whom He entrusted the conversion of the gentiles, however, the Lord called fishermen,[27] and their leader was Peter, who was to be a fisher for Rome, the mistress of the gentiles, as though for whales in the ocean.

Christ, however, who said that He was sent only to the lost sheep of the house of Israel, claimed for himself the title not of fisherman, but of shepherd.

Chapter Six

Now also becomes clear the solution of the question which for a long time has tormented interpreters of this book: why on the second day Moses did not say "And God saw that it was good." If we say what is usually said, that it was not done because the work of the waters was not completed on that day but on the third, when the waters under the heavens flowed to-

25 I Corinthians 9:1-12.

26 The Biblical reference is John 2:14, but the basis of this interpretation is uncertain.

27 Matthew 4:19.

gether into one place, it will scarcely seem fully satisfactory. The peculiar work of the second day is not the disposition of the waters but of the firmament, which was set in the midst of the waters. On that day were sufficiently completed both the making of the firmament, when God said "Let there be a firmament made," and the division of the waters, when he said "And let it divide the waters from the waters." The gathering of the waters, which is called the sea, and the uncovering of the earth, and the generation of the plants have the pattern of a wholly different work, and therefore they were accomplished on another day, the third, to which they pertained.

Therefore the explanation of a deeper mystery must be sought. The firmament (as we showed above) represents the law. And the firmament was in a sense unformed and simply not finished until it was furnished with the sun, moon, and stars, just as the law was not indeed bad (as the Manicheans say), but simply not good or perfect until Christ came to fulfill it. If the firmament had been bad, it would not have accepted the sun; if it had been good, it would not have needed it. But the firmament was good insofar as it was capable of receiving the sun and the other stars, just as the law was good insofar as it taught us of Christ; and on account of the crudity of his people, Moses allowed many things which the Gospel did not allow later.

Although we cannot call the law bad, as Mani believed, nevertheless we cannot call it good, as is clearly taught by the prophet according to whom God, speaking of the Hebrews, says, "I gave them statutes that were not good,"[28] that is, not perfected, not complete, not finished. This is confirmed by the ancient Hebrew doctors who, interpreting the passage of Ecclesiastes, "Vanity of vanities, and all is vanity,"[29] say that even the law is vain until the Messiah comes.

And so much for this.

[28] Ezekiel 20:25.
[29] Ecclesiastes 1:2.

Chapter Seven

It was the supreme gift of the incarnate Word that through the sacrament of baptism, by which the virtue of Christ is transfused into us, we may be reborn as sons of God, born not of the blood, but of God. Moses finally shows us this when, after the sun has risen and been shown to the world, and after the fertilization of the waters and the land, he makes man in the image of God, not earthly man, but the heavenly. After the gentiles and the Jews had been converted to Christ, it remained for them, shaping themselves to the cross of the Lord through the holy bath, to be re-made in the image of God. For if baptism makes men sons of God, and the son is the image of the Father, is not the virtue of the whole Trinity as it operates in baptism expressed in the words "Let us make man to our image"? Therefore, if we are in the image of God, we are also in that of the Son. If we are sons and heirs, we are heirs of God and co-heirs with Christ. But who are the sons? It is written by Paul that we cry *abba* (father) in the Holy Spirit.[30]

Therefore those who live in the Spirit are sons of God and brothers of Christ, predestined for the eternal inheritance which they will happily possess in the heavenly Jerusalem as the reward of faith and of life well lived.

[30] Romans 8:15; Galatians 4:6.

EXPOSITION OF THE FIRST PHRASE: "IN THE BEGINNING"

Now we have come to the end of our work, having gone through the sevenfold interpretation of the entire text. But I know that we have hitherto left something untouched and undiscussed which it seems we should have explained at the very first, that is, what is meant by the first phrase of the law, "In the beginning." Neither rashly, however, nor without reason have I chosen to speak of this beginning at the end of the whole work. I am not here going to discuss the Son of God, who is the beginning through which all things were made (for he is the wisdom of the Father), nor shall I prove here that the ancient Hebrews thought as we do, for I shall do this elsewhere. But I intend, through another system of interpretation, to give my readers a taste of Mosaic profundity.

I shall not do this until we have deliberated a little on a certain dogma which is truly a paradox of the earlier Hebrew learning. It is the firm opinion of all the ancients, unanimously asserted as beyond doubt, that the five books of the Mosaic law contain the entire knowledge of all arts and wisdom both divine and human. This knowledge is hidden and concealed, however, in the very letters of which the phrases of the law are composed. How this is so, we shall now demonstrate.

Let us take as an example the first part of the book of Genesis, from the beginning to the place where it is written: "And God saw the light, that it was good." This whole passage is composed of 103 letters, which, arranged as they are, make up the words which we read, displaying nothing but the common and trivial. But this arrangement of letters, this text, composes the shell of a secret kernel of hidden mysteries. If we open up the words and take the same letters separately and, according to the rules which the Hebrews hand down, join them together properly into the sayings that can be made up of them, they

say that there will appear to us, if we are fit for hidden wisdom,
many wise and wonderful doctrines. If this is done with the
whole law, there will finally be brought to light by the proper
placing and connecting of its elements all learning and the
secrets of all the liberal disciplines. I said, however, if we are fit
for hidden wisdom. It can happen that in our pulling and tearing apart and putting together of some expressions, many words
may be spawned, and we may give birth to a manifold train of
discourse which may teach and signify great things; but unless
one has pursued the study of them elsewhere, he may fail to
understand what these things mean and therefore may despise
them as useless and accidental.

We cannot learn dogmas and doctrines here; we can only
recognize them. I cannot prove or demonstrate what I claim,
since I neither have made a test of it nor have confidence of
being able to make one; but I do not deny or despise this theory,
partly because it has mighty supporters, and partly because
even greater things can easily be believed of Moses, who was
acquainted with the whole house of God. I thought, however,
that it would not be displeasing to men of our time if I made
public display of the gems, richer than those which the poets
say the Hermus and Pactolus bear,[1] which presented themselves
to me as I skirted the shore of this sea without even entering
its depths.

Applying the rules of the ancients to the first phrase of the
work, which is read *Beresit* by the Hebrews and "In the beginning" by us, I wanted to see whether I too could bring to
light something worth knowing. Beyond my hope and expecta-
tion I found what I myself did not believe as I found it, and
what others will not believe easily: the whole plan of the creation of the world and of all things in it disclosed and explained
in that one phrase.

I am saying a wonderful thing, incredible and unheard of.
You will soon believe it, however, if you pay attention, and the
facts themselves will prove me right.

Among the Hebrews, this phrase is written thus: בראשית,

1 Fabled rivers of golden sands in ancient Lydia.

berescith. From this, if we join the third letter to the first, comes the word אב, *ab.* If we add the second to the doubled first, we get בבר, *bebar.* If we read all except the first, we get ראשית, *resith.* If we connect the fourth to the first and last, we get שבת, *sciabat.* If we take the first three in the order in which they come, we get ברא, *bara.* If, leaving out the first, we take the next three, we get ראש, *rosc.* If, leaving out the first and second, we take the two following, we get אש, *es.* If, leaving out the first three, we join the fourth to the last, we get שת, *seth.* Again, if we join the second to the first, we get רב, *rab.* If after the third we set the fifth and fourth, we get איש, *hisc.* If we join the first two to the last two, we get ברית, *berith.* If we add the last to the first, we get the twelfth and last word, which is תב, *thob,* the *thau* being changed into the letter *thet,* which is very common in Hebrew.

Let us see first what these words mean in Latin, then what mysteries of all nature they reveal to those not ignorant of philosophy. *Ab* means "the father"; *bebar* "in the son" and "through the son" (for the prefix *beth* means both); *resit,* "the beginning"; *sabath,* "the rest and end"; *bara,* "created"; *rosc,* "head"; *es,* "fire"; *seth,* "foundation"; *rab,* "of the great"; *hisc,* "of the man"; *berit,* "with a pact"; *thob,* "with good." If we fit the whole passage together following this order, it will read like this: "The father, in the Son and through the Son, the beginning and end or rest, created the head, the fire, and the foundation of the great man with a good pact." This whole passage results from taking apart and putting together that first word.

How deep and full of all learning its meaning is can by no means be plain to all. But at least some, if not all, of what these words signify to us is clear to all. All Christians know what is meant by saying that the Father created in and through the Son, and likewise what is meant by saying that the Son is the beginning and end of all things. For He is Alpha and Omega (as John writes),[2] and He called himself the beginning, and we have shown that He is the end of all things, in which they are

2 The Apocalypse (Revelation) 1:8.

restored to their beginning. The rest is a little more obscure, namely, what the head, the fire, and the foundation of the great man refer to, what the pact may be, and why it is called good. It is not easy for everyone to see immediately that here is explained the whole plan, relationship, and felicity, which we treated last of all, of the four worlds that we have discussed.

In the first place, therefore, it should be noticed that the world is what Moses calls "the great man." For if man is a little world, then certainly the world is a great man.

Taking opportunity from this, he appropriately represents the three worlds, the intellectual, the heavenly, and the corruptible, by the three parts of man, by this metaphor not only indicating that all the worlds are contained in man, but also stating briefly which part of man corresponds to which world.

Therefore let us consider the three parts of man: the highest is the head; then that which stretches from the neck to the navel; thirdly, that which extends from the navel to the feet. These parts of the human figure are divided and separated by a certain diversity. But it is wonderful how beautifully and how perfectly, in the most precise manner, they correspond respectively to the three parts of the world.

In the head is the brain, the fountain of knowledge. In the breast is the heart, the fountain of motion, life, and heat. In the lowest part are the genitals, the principle of generation. Likewise in the world the highest part, which is the angelic or intellectual world, is the fountain of knowledge, because that nature was made for understanding. The middle part, which is the sky, is the principle of life, motion, and heat, in which the sun rules as the heart does in the breast. Below the moon, as all know, is the principle of generation and corruption. You see how aptly all these parts of the world and of man correspond. Moses designated the first by its proper name, the head. The second, however, he called fire, because by this name many refer to the sky, and because in us this part is the principle of heat. The third he called the foundation, because (as all know) the whole human body is begun and sustained by it. He added that God created these with a good pact, because the law of

God's wisdom decreed among them a pact of peace and friendship in conformity with the kinship and mutual harmony of
their natures. This pact is good, therefore, because it is directed
and oriented toward God, who is the good itself, so that just as
within itself the whole world is one, so also it is, in the end,
one with its Maker.

Let us also copy the holy pact of the world, so that we may be
united together in mutual charity, and that at the same time,
through the true love of God, we may all achieve our felicity
and become one with Him.